SOULS OF LEGENDS SPEAK

SOULS OF LEGENDS SPEAK

Surprising Reflections from the Other Side

SANDY COWEN

Waterside Productions

www.sandycowen.com

The messages from the deceased were received through the method of channeling through a clairaudient medium. That medium is not responsible for the contents of the messages, only for the accurate and faithful transcription of them.

Printed in the United States of America

First Printing, 2021

ISBN-13: 978-1-956503-30-2 print edition
ISBN-13: 978-1-956503-31-9 ebook edition

Waterside Productions
2055 Oxford Ave
Cardiff, CA 92007
www.waterside.com

To my son, Jon, who has been an inspiration to so many on the "other side" and, of course, to me.

TABLE OF CONTENTS

INTRODUCTION

When I buy a book, I routinely start reading right away and I'm always thrilled to jump into the first chapter. What is off-putting is when first I'm confronted with a lengthy introduction. So, readers, breathe a sigh of relief because that won't happen here. I'll only be sharing the most critical elements of the backstory.

Souls from the "other side" come to me frequently, yet I'm not a commercial medium. Instead, I'm a clairaudient who hears the messages and transcribes every single word to capture the nuances and preserve the content. I guess you could consider me a spiritual secretary. I'm not a channel who goes into a trance and speaks in the language of the sender, instead I'm given these messages telepathically and then transcribe their thoughts with the vocabulary I have at hand. They trust me with this, which is why they've kept coming and that's why this book will be conversational and easy to read. I explain more on that later.

Over the years, every message I've ever received has been transcribed and filed away. I have never solicited any visitors to come—they just show up after signaling me first, through a variety of ways. This unusual process began more than thirty years ago but I kept it secret until the passing of my only child, my forty-eight-year-old son Jon in 2018. Now, I'm "out of the closet," so to speak.

Like I said, for three decades I've received hundreds of messages, but not necessarily from the rich and famous. They were more ordinary souls that were familiar to me and of course, the Divine. However, since "*Hi Momma, It's Me*", my last book, the number of legendary figures showing up has been overwhelming with one hundred and twenty-four making themselves known in a few short months. They were all "big deals" in their lives, and I was in awe of the wisdom, insight, and the reflections they so openly shared. They came with no ego, no ulterior motive, and no posturing—just a sincere desire to reveal what they'd learned, to support my work and hopefully to contribute to mankind one more time. Their messages were too meaningful to simply file away, so *Souls of Legends Speak* was born.

Now, some of you might be skeptical and assume this book is fiction; it is not. If you read carefully, it will be impossible to ignore the authenticity of the content. You'll find their comments unique with many being extremely profound. You might also recognize that their personalities seem to have remained intact.

I hope you'll recognize the privilege you've been given to peek into the lives of some of the most famous people of all time. If you're a notetaker or one who highlights the pages of a book, you'll want to have a pen or highlighting tool nearby to capture the brilliance and quotes you'll want to repeat or remember. They are too amazing for any one author to be clever enough to create, especially since this book was written or compiled in five months.

Readers may also find, occasionally, these souls referencing my son, Jon, since he's become somewhat of an example over there. Jon's recent soul growth clearly illustrates the benefits of actively connecting across dimensions. In Jon's case, immediately after his passing, the mother/son relationship was rekindled, and our relationship flourished. The result has been Jon's continued spiritual blossoming and, of course, my healing. Our connection also provides a vehicle for my son to make amends, offer comfort to loved ones and help repair some of the damage he may have caused in his past relationships.

It seems many souls have also noticed Jon's current activity level. In fact, he's pretty busy on that side as he pokes, prods and coaches souls around him to continue to reach out to their loved ones. Funny, really, I'm encouraging people to open to the possibility of such connecting on this side and he is doing his "thing" on the other side—sort of a push-pull effect. It appears we're some pair!

So, needless to say, my mission for the remainder of my life and the reason for the previous book, *"Hi Momma, It's Me"* as well as this book,

Souls of Legends Speak, is to let people know that their loved ones are not that far away, that connecting across dimensions *is* possible, and that living in unconditional love makes the entire process effortless.

I am most grateful to the souls who participated in this book and allowed me to receive their messages. I'm now very eager to share them with you.

Chapter 1

AND HERE THEY COME!

It wasn't long after my previous book, "*Hi Momma, It's Me*", was published that unique and interesting souls from the other side began coming to me in droves. That process started in mid-summer 2020 and accelerated into late spring 2021. First, it was Henry Ford and then Spencer Tracy, Mickey Mantle and Jimi Hendrix. Within another week I heard from Golda Meir, Elisabeth Kübler-Ross, Paul Harvey and Billy Graham. It was an odd collection of souls which I never would have thought of assembling, yet there they were.

I was struck by the sheer volume, but also by the level of accomplishment from each of the people who showed up; they were all legendary. That phenomenon had to be triggered by something, and I've come to realize that "*Hi Momma, It's Me*" was the catalyst. That personal and intimate book talked about two things: how souls stay connected forever and the power of undying love. Both messages seemed to resonate with those who have departed and there was no question I was receiving their support.

When "*Hi Momma, It's Me*" was published, it was a physical demonstration of my commitment to becoming a messenger for those on the other side. That book also shared in the most meaningful part, the story of how my son, Jon, and I reconnected only hours after his passing in 2018 and have continued our ongoing relationship. I believe the process Jon and I are experiencing, as well as the benefits we each received, was a surprise to many departed souls.

The rewards I received from Jon and my connection were enormous and obvious for me. I felt less grief and was able to heal more quickly from his physical loss. The comfort of knowing that Jon was nearby, and his frequent messages brought me enormous peace and finally, joy.

Not surprisingly, Jon received benefits as well. Through our ongoing connection, he has been able to actively make amends, talk through some of his soul-based learnings and offer support and love to me in a concrete way, giving him the ability to repay me through his gratitude and new expressions of love that he hadn't always managed to convey. It also appears that through this continual dialogue between us, Jon's soul experiences more rapid healing and a purification which helps raise his soul's frequency or ability to radiate even more love. Those factors have been noticed by souls on the other side.

What has been happening to Jon isn't a figment of my imagination or assumption on my part since, besides Jon's recount, I've also heard our relationship described by many of the new souls who've come to me and repeatedly shed even more light on this phenomenon. They could instantly relate to the benefits of connecting and were eager to reach out in their own way, too. Some wanted to be helpful to humanity once more, while others were eager to receive additional revelations regarding their own issues by merely having someone with whom to talk things through; an option not available over there.

Paul Harvey, for example, was able to articulate most concisely why the ability for them to connect with those of us still alive is so advantageous to souls now departed. Therefore, I'd like to share his statement in its entirety.

Paul Harvey was also very succinct, which should come as no surprise to those of you who ever listened to his radio broadcasts. He always revealed the fascinating and unknown story behind either a famous name or famous event. As you'll see, Paul Harvey hasn't lost his touch

PAUL HARVEY

(1918–2009) ABC News radio broadcaster whose commentaries appeared throughout the day reaching twenty-four million people per week. He was best known for his "The Rest of the Story" segments.

Did I catch you at a good time? Good. I haven't had the opportunity to speak out for a while. Glad you're taking this down. ☺ *I want to address your book ["Hi Momma, It's Me"] and the need for it. Maybe my perspective will make sense to some people.*

When this life on earth ends, there is a reckoning. There's always a reckoning for misdeeds and bad behavior. In this case we're over here when we become aware of our wrong doings, sometimes committed out of ignorance or that fog of ego and determination that makes us oblivious to anything or anyone who gets in our way. As I said, we become aware and then what? We may relive the pain others felt but all that does is make us aware of the depth of our depravity or indifference. It does nothing to correct the wrong.

So, what then? We decide to return to another life so we can correct the error of our ways by somehow living a life that makes up for what we did, or if we were slow learners, to make us experience the same pain from others in order to "get it." A lengthy process to be sure.

What you are doing Sandy, is providing the <u>*only*</u> [immediate] *opportunity we have to express unending gratitude to those who truly helped us in this life and to make amends, directly, to those we wronged. You shorten the period of time needed* [for our souls] *to progress.*

Now, ugliness committed on a mass scale to hundreds, thousands or millions can't be dealt with directly this way—case in point, Hitler. They pay through never, or practically never, being able to experience the joy/love they passed through before their life review process began here. But for all others, who yearn to reach out and express their sorrow and regret, your books on connecting open the doors to that possibility! Do you know how massive that effort is?

We are all thrilled with your work and amazed at your son's growth since your relationship across dimensions began. Jon is an example, and you are our angel!!!

Sandy, I hope you'll include me in your next book. You are a voice for the voiceless souls here, you're blessed beyond words and God has anointed this work. We're here to help and thank you for giving me a venue once again to bring people the "Rest of the Story…"

Forever a friend, Paul Harvey

The gift of communicating externally was something these souls had thought was lost to them, unless they chose to return to life, in another experience. Most all processes offered in Heaven are internal in nature unless souls reach out to "this side." Many had tried to connect with loved ones and friends over the years but very few, if any, were ever able to make that connection. Most friends and loved ones they wanted to reach were too busy or distracted to be open enough to receive. Sad really, since typically all these souls wanted to convey was how sorry they were for any wrong they'd caused, how much they wanted to reassure loved ones that they were now at peace, or simply to offer love and support. Now, with this book, they feel there's the possibility to be productive once again and perhaps help people who are still living.

Flashback to the Beginning

Before we rush too far ahead with all these incredible messages, let me explain a little about the method by which these souls connect with me, and then how I commit their communications to pen and paper. It's a fascinating process.

As always, when I become a conduit for what souls on the other side have to say, they let me know. I have never specifically invited any of them to come, but there seems to be an open-door policy already established. They'd be stacked up for miles if there wasn't a system of signals I've learned to recognize; signals I can't ignore. They use energy, technology, and electronics to reach me—or rather, to get my attention. The result? Working on my computer, watching television and texting are anything but routine in my world. Smoke alarms and security alarms go off, my doorbell rings; and my phone has even called other people, without me nearby. The only way I found out about one phone call was when the person I supposedly dialed, returned the call. This random man pushed the button to return a call and I answered. Their options are limitless if their attempts are energy-based: streetlights flash and electronics in my car act bizarrely, too. So, needless to say, my life is extraordinary, unpredictable and I'm rarely ever bored.

Let me share one very memorable connection. It was a winter morning when I was awakened at 5 AM, still pitch black in Arizona, by a bright light in my bedroom that startled me from a dead sleep. That light came from my closed wooden armoire, in which a flatscreen TV sits, that I turn off every evening. I also routinely shut both wooden doors to protect myself against the energy that emanates from electronics, even when they're turned off. Anyway, the armoire door has inserts of chicken wire and a lovely fabric gathered behind them on the center panel of each door. That specific morning, the television switched on and the light instantly penetrated the fabric and even the cracks around the doors. What I saw was a blinding VISEO logo I'd never seen before. VISEO happens to be the brand of my television. Well, the VISEO logo bears a resemblance to Superman's logo, which I thought was particularly funny. That wouldn't't have been a big deal except I couldn't turn the TV or logo off. I used the remote device, accessed the television directly and finally unplugged the TV from the wall—the logo still didn't disappear. Finally, I grabbed a couple very thick, plush towels, double-folded them, and draped them over the television and shut the doors. Whew! A reprieve for a bit until I could take a breath and begin my day.

A few minutes later I realized that I'd better check to see who the visitor was, so maybe the logo would disappear more quickly. There was no question that someone from the other side had been trying to contact me. When I asked, it wasn't just one soul reaching out, or two, or three or even four, it was five. All of them addressing the same subject and each with their own but equally profound spin. You'll read about them later but that turned out to be a very busy day. Now, you're beginning to get an idea of how complicated my life can be. Explaining what happens with my computer could be a chapter unto itself.

Back to the Rush of Souls

After "*Hi Momma, It's Me*" was published, more and more souls excitedly came but now their messages were different. Having realized the benefit to them to connect with us, they began to share more. Through this process they hoped others still living could learn from their experiences and they'd be able to contribute, once again. Secondly, I believe they thought vocalizing their regrets and lessons to someone else could provide additional insights, like Paul Harvey described. Finally, in some way, their sharing might could be a vehicle through which they'd be able to indirectly make amends and accelerate their own soul's purification. Others just wanted to offer me support, while they slipped in something reflective about their own amazing lives.

First twenty, then forty, then fifty souls came, and by the time I began to recognize the staggering number, I also realized this needed to be another book. So, like always, I wrote down every single word I heard, so as not to miss one single nuance. I filter nothing, I interject nothing, and what you will read throughout this book is pure and uncensored.

As the months passed, I received well over one hundred new messages from very famous people. When I began to question why so many *big names* were appearing, that was explained to me too, since I was afraid people would not believe this amazing assemblage.

As you might begin to realize, these souls always explain everything far better than I, so once again, I'm deferring to the wisdom from beyond to help bring clarity in a way everyone can easily understand. The best explanation of the VIP rush came from Lee Iacocca. Lee expounded on a few other personal points as well, but he did manage to provide a clear interpretation of why only famous voices were the ones stepping up to participate in this book. This is what he said:

LEE IACOCCA

(1924–2019) An American automobile executive best known for the development of the Ford Mustang and Ford Pinto cars while at Ford Motor Company and then for reviving the Chrysler Corporation.

Sandy, my friend,

OK if I call you that? Everybody up here feels they know you because you are a light to help mankind. What I mean by that is you're the funnel by which we can, again, reach mankind with what we know.

No matter how small a person's life in comparison to gigantic, visual lives like some who have already come to you, we all learn the same lessons when we incarnate on earth to grow. Same lessons. But who is going to pay attention to what Fred Jones of Philadelphia tells us? No one, frankly. But myself? Winston Churchill? Barry Goldwater? Totally different story. Yet, Fred and I have the same unperfected soul yearning to become complete in love so we can rest for all eternity like Jon says, "with the big dogs."

Lee's reference to my son Jon's description of Ascended Masters appeared in my last book, "*Hi Momma, It's Me*". In that book, when I asked Jon if he had seen Jesus, he explained that although souls can see and sometimes brush into those of a higher frequency such as Ascended Masters, his own energy wasn't pure enough to "hang with the big dogs." At first, I gasped thinking Jon's comment was sacrilege, but later I found that everyone over there thought it was funny, even God. Yes, God does have a sense of humor. So, many who have come to me have referred to Jon's descriptor, with a smile.

Clever, your son. You two are quite the pair and he seems to beam when we all reach out to you. He knows your talent and that we are in pure, selfless, and capable hands.

So, what are we all sharing? I've taken the lead here to explain it. Surprised? Anyway, as we speak through you, we gain more insight as to our own discoveries and imperfections. You know how sometimes when we're confused about a complex issue with no likely solution, just talking out loud sometimes sheds light on the answer. It's like releasing air from the valve of an overinflated tire – then it runs more smoothly on the uneven surface of the road. Of course, I'd give a car analogy.

Speaking through you allows us to do the same. To share important thoughts to help others perfect their lives more quickly and with ease on earth while, at the same time, providing us additional insight so we can reflect again on our lives to recognize the pain we may have caused others and to find forgiveness of self. All for faster soul growth and increasing the purity of our frequency.

I think I over-explain – but always did that. ☺ You are one hundred percent right when you say this process can reduce the lives spent in reincarnation by up to one half.

Let me say more about that. Most, in fact all, reincarnation is not for punishment; it is for waking us up to a deeper understanding of others and how we can be of service to help; our own shortcomings so we can learn to forgive; or for us to play, sometimes painful roles to help another's growth or discovery.

Those who volunteer for the last one are truly saints because the pain is so bad. Unless they're protected by the cloak of physical traits or weaknesses that mask the reality of what they're charged to do: addiction, mental disease or defect, physical disease, or defect, etc.

As glorious as we may think another's life is—ha—it's always [filled with] *more pain or challenges than we could know! So, you're right again to teach not to judge others, ever. Avoid maybe, but judging is an ignorant process.*

Well, my dear Sandy, I've rattled on enough. Reminds me of the old days when somebody really cared about my opinion! Thank you for being there. Thank you for helping us and thank you for your wonderful work. All the energy we can muster is being sent your way, with bushels of— oops, pick-up trucks full of love!

Leaving while I'm ahead. Your friend, forever—Lee

With the wonderful explanations from Paul Harvey and Lee Iacocca, I don't have to offer much more; we can just jump right into the brilliant and profound messages that await. I tried to categorize chapters based on their overall content and believe that will make readers more eager to digest the messages section by section. Some are messages that can be read quickly, but others require a slow, deliberate absorption. Most of the time, I've included the entire message with a greeting and closing - since a few are surprising.

I believe you'll find, as I did, that the personalities of these icons have remained intact and the flavor of who they were seems to come through as they speak. I've provided very little commentary as I weave those soul-mail messages together throughout this book. The only time I say much is to elaborate on a comment of theirs about something personal between us, to explain a situation they've picked-up in my energy field that relates to them, or to praise something about their delivery such as how incredibly honest, free of ego and transparent many are in sharing their lives, their feelings, and their regrets.

One more clarification is needed. Since some of these souls have deep scientific or professional knowledge, their commentary is limited by my vocabulary, which a couple of the souls masterfully explain. Again, to clarify, I am not a channel, using a trance state to communicate verbally; I am more of a spiritual secretary. I'm a clairaudient, hearing thoughts telepathically and those thoughts are transcribed by me through the limits of the vocabulary I have at my disposal. They may send a complex thought to me, but I am never asked to relay technical or scientific detail. We talk about the forest, rarely the trees. The same process applies to different languages, dialects or common phrases used many generations ago.

Many have said they are grateful for my total objectivity in the process and for keeping pure to their intent, without my own ego's involvement. Still, when you hear from them—even souls who lived millenniums ago—the reason you can easily understand the messages is that they communicate the thought and I put those thoughts into words. So far, everybody seems happy.

As you read through this book, you'll find some messages make a brief reference to something personal they know about me that involves them in some way. I thought this element of their commentary was uncanny: *How could they know that?* I'd think. It appears that common experiences between a particular soul and the person living is revealed in our energy field as they reach out. They comment on those compatible or actual events generally with humor and delight. In other cases, some reference my son, Jon, and how they observe him or his soul growth. They explain it all better than I do so there is no need for me to say more.

I hope all the incredible array of messages shared in the following chapters will help you gain a better understanding of what the afterlife holds. Perhaps it will make it possible to see our world from a new perspective and learn lessons from their lives that can enrich yours. If nothing else, you'll be able to reconnect once more with icons you admired but who you believed were lost forever. They are not.

Chapter 2

REFLECTIONS ON A UNIQUE LIFE

When we reach the other side, we're all given the opportunity to reflect on our lives and very often only then, do we begin to recognize our misdeeds and the pain we caused others. You've all heard the expression that our lives pass before us; well, it appears that's exactly what happens. But it doesn't happen in a flash—this process takes a very, very long time.

My son, Jon, summed it up the best when he came to visit in April 2021. He said that he's still looking back on his life and learning the obvious first, the more subtle next, and then the nuances. Some pain-causing actions are direct and easily recognizable, yet others are more emotion-based and those feelings result in coloring our personalities, which can be equally harmful. We may hurt communities of souls with our indifference, disrespect, resentment or in passing judgment, for example.

Every life is complicated, but many are routine in nature; we're born and die, and, in the middle, we follow our life path through friendships, family dynamics, successes and failures in our health challenges and those of others, as well as professional, emotional, and spiritual struggles. There are a million variations of those but not all lives represent the extremes you'll read about next. The lives these legends had to endure were not only magnified by their celebrity, but their individual journeys contained extraordinarily unique challenges.

Here you will find a well-known entertainer. *This* one was not only the most popular entertainer in the world during the peak of his career but was also perceived by some to be a pedophile. Next, although there are a handful of famous names who studied animals in the wild, this was the only one brutally murdered at her mountain camp. Others included a member of one widely celebrated family who couldn't deal with her self-described inferiority, and finally, a man who was one of the greatest thinkers in our time but was also almost totally restricted by his physical helplessness.

Although each of these lives was renowned, every one of them took an unexpected twist. The fascinating part is how they now perceive those lives and the candid nature and objectivity with which they share with us. What's fascinating to me is the lack of ego and defensive posturing that exists now. Ah, the purity of our souls once we reach Heaven!

MICHAEL JACKSON

(1958–2009) Legendary American singer, songwriter, and dancer, dubbed the "King of Pop." Jackson was one of the most significant cultural figures of the twentieth century.

Hi there, Sandy.

I'm Michael, and I know you know who I am. I'm a little timid about coming to you because, as talented as I was, I had a very screwed-up life.

My father was not a great dad. I believe he loved us, in his own way, but I was confused how he demonstrated that love. A harsh disciplinarian, heavy on the work ethic and no consideration of our emotions or souls. No wonder I had no idea what love looked like or what a childhood looked like. We may have simply been in a work camp, somewhere.

I wanted love, I needed love, as we all do, but everyone around me wanted something from me in some form. I couldn't trust anyone but the young and innocent. I wasn't aroused by them—I was desperate for closeness, intimacy, and love in any pure form. Plus, all of my fantasies fulfilled my need for a childhood, or one I imagined was real.

My fallback was always my craft, so I didn't give my work or engage my talent 100 percent, it was lived 250 percent. Totally abnormal. In a world without trust or love, I found security in work, and peace in sleeping; which I had to induce always, and much more drastically in later years.

Now I'm here and I believe I hurt others, which I've been realizing but I even have to learn here to grasp that. I was totally naïve and innocent. Being in God's presence is so magical, so wondrous, so glorious. I have friends here who I know truly loved me, like Elizabeth [Taylor]. *I am wrapped in Divine peace and beginning to feel what real, unconditional love is like.*

I won't be back for a bit because I need to absorb the reality of love before I return and am able to give it to others. What I gave youngsters was not love. It was desperation, curiosity, and some sense of voyeurism that I pieced together from my meager repertoire of options.

I'm here as an example, Sandy. No ego anymore—just to warn parents to love the souls of their children and not the shell or expression of talent its housed in. And, to warn audiences that the celebrities they see and in some instances worship, aren't any more perfect or complete than they are, [and] *sometimes are much more tragic.*

So, admire the talent and see the rest of them with a gentleness and compassion they'd give any stranger they meet who might have issues, too. Performers are not products—they're all human and the love they seek, you all can give with unselfish and open hearts, just as Sandy talks about.

I wished I'd have known you, Sandy. I think you'd have seen who I was instantly, and I'd have known that. Bless you and your work. We all need you doing your magic over there.

Thank you for this forum to express, again. This time, from the soul level, Michael

DIAN FOSSEY

(1932–1985) American primatologist and conservationist known for her study, in the mountain forests of Rwanda, of mountain gorilla groups. She was eventually murdered. Her book *Gorillas in the Midst* was adapted into a 1988 film of the same name.

Sandy – I know I'm a surprise coming to you "out of the midst." Ha! I couldn't resist.

You are as courageous as I was. Seeing something from afar that frightened many and reaching out to them with love, not to commercialize that contact but to bring a clearer understanding of them to all.

I'm not sure I could compare her life communicating with gorillas to my life communicating with the glorious souls on the other side, still, I guess we both consider our subjects beautiful and more than worthy of our efforts.

We aren't dissimilar, are we? I know you couldn't imagine who I was, but Google was good. Glad you didn't mix me up with Jane Goodall; we were different. I was a pioneer and a voice to make people more aware of these glorious creatures and took everything to the next step. Like you, always a pioneer who sees things before others, works in silence and seclusion and [is] *setting the stage for others to become more famous. You've done that over your life, haven't you?*

I've been constantly amazed throughout this process how these souls intuit elements of my life just by simply connecting with me from "over there." Dian's reference to "setting the stage for others to become more famous" was one such reference. Ironically, I've done much of that in my life, and as visible as I was in the local community, accomplishments I delivered behind the scenes made it possible for others to rise to more prominence statewide and nationally —in political circles, the nonprofit world and in growing their own businesses. Always big achievements but the resulting rewards were reaped by others. Still, I was content with seeing the results, not grabbing the spotlight. Dian somehow knew that and related.

Now, we have all the souls up here supporting us and I have all my magnificent gorillas at every stage of their being from the very first to most current. Amazing! And I'm still in awe of them.

Dian was referring to her Second Heaven experience in this paragraph. Although I've dedicated another entire chapter to this Heavenly phenomenon, her quote is retained here to give you a glimpse of what's to follow.

The Second Heaven, along with the Heaven we all typically picture, is a place to enjoy and relive this life's greatest passion and the scope of that experience isn't limited to what you may have observed in your own life, but what existed well before and beyond. This concept was covered in depth in my previous book "*Hi Momma, It's Me.*"

The final reflection on the tragic end of Dian's life and her brutal death, was likely at the hands of the poachers against whom she had fought for decades. She was killed at her camp in the forest of the Virunga Mountains in Rwanda.

My death was meant to be so I could step away for others. No animosity, not even fear surrounding it. I just knew. I was always alone (or felt alone) in my life, but my heart and soul reached out to other souls who needed a voice. Guess those were my gorillas!

Welcome to my world, Sandy. Now, you're my sister. Dian

MARGAUX HEMINGWAY

(1954–1996) American fashion model and actress who was also the granddaughter of writer Ernest Hemingway. She earned

success as a supermodel in the mid-1970's appearing on the covers of *Cosmopolitan*, *Elle*, *Harper's Bazaar*, *Vogue*, and *TIME*. She committed suicide.

Hello, Sandy.

My name is Margaux. I am probably the least known and least talented of the Hemingway family. People must think it is great to be part of a famous family, but it is quite the opposite.

The legend always has his or her clear niche in history, purely defined and oozing with some very obvious talent. The rest of us bob around in the wake of that infamy not knowing who we are, what we are or where we are going. In this sea of uncertainty, we're supposed to build a healthy life and be satisfied living in the shadow without sunlight flooding down onto us. It's hard, very hard. We can't mimic without coming up very short, and in any [other] *career we attempt the expectations are sky high.*

I was miserable, beautiful somehow, but miserable. Add to that any weakness in our genes that manifested in health issues are expected to be quickly identified and satisfied so the family legacy is not disturbed.

I believe the *weakness in our genes* to which Margaux referred was either a reference to the epilepsy, which plagued her since age seven, or the reason non-prescribed drugs were found at her bedside and a lethal dose in her system that was well beyond the therapeutic range. Her suicide or accidental overdose happened on the anniversary of her grandfather's death.

I believe I still hold some anger as to my lot in life and I'm working hard on that. Life is always a lesson of sorts. I'm trying to grasp that all and although I've been gone a while, it takes many (in your years) to even realize what our path was. At least it is that way for me.

I came [for your book] *to show people how pure reflection, without attachment or expectation, can help us heal more quickly.*

Everyone still living should try to do some of that early to allow for more time to bask in bliss here.

This life on earth, or elsewhere, is to learn and grow, to refine and polish until we are more Christ-like or God-like, if one prefers. No judgment surrounding those who exercise this discipline while living, only applause from here.

I hope I helped someone. Margaux

This next message is from someone who, as he aged, lost his ability to walk, then could move only a muscle or two, eventually to the point where he could not speak. He still managed to marry twice, father children and draw the attention of the entire world with his brilliance. What lesson from him could we possibility relate to? You'll see.

STEPHEN HAWKING

(1942–2018) English theoretical physicist, cosmologist, and author who was the Lucasian Professor of Mathematics at the University of Cambridge from 1979-2009 and the director of research at the Centre for Theoretical Cosmology, also at Cambridge, when he died.

Hi Sandy –

I think you're afraid to take this message for fear you won't get it right! Nonsense. You're the best one to write to. I won't get technical or stay in the weeds. This is about life, not math and science.

Resilience, that's what I'm here to talk about. I guess I was a great example of that.

It makes no difference one's lot in life, one's disabilities – physically, mentally, or emotionally. God gave each of us at least one gift and often a blend. My life was merely an example of what one can do if we accept what we're given and then embrace the gifts that are possible for us to pursue.

If your body is weak, your mind may be strong, like mine. If you're dyslexic or have trouble with the concrete tools of learning, unleash your creativity. No vision? Use your voice. No mental strength? Use your body's gifts. Stay focused on the positive. Strive for mastery that satisfies yourself, no one else. Your life will end up being an example, an inspiration and perhaps you'll produce one-of-a-kind solutions for problems, inventions to ease our lives, physical feats that make people gasp, or beauty that stops others dead in their tracks.

Never feel like a victim. Bless your life – in all forms and surprise yourself every day by how much you've still accomplished.

I'm Stephen Hawking and I was resilient. Leaving you with a challenge.—SH

Chapter 3

WOMEN'S BATTLE FOR CREDIBILITY

Women have continually struggled for equality: for their right to have a voice and opinion, their right to enter the workplace and succeed, as well as their right to vote. Eventually the battle focused on the right to be paid equally for workplace contribution. Most women over time simply wanted some level of respect and to be recognized for the size of their brain instead of the size of their bra. Throughout history, women have had to fight when they wanted to step into their own power.

The extraordinary females selected for this section represent diverse societies and areas of interest that span the last five hundred years. Each of these women specifically referenced the challenges she faced in a way that expressed exactly who she was in this last life and in a way to which many of us can totally relate to today.

What I thought was significant was how these four women saw their lives at the time and how the lessons each reference may still be applicable in our current world. The surprising voice, represented last, clears up one very public and long-standing question that has plagued and fascinated many of us since 1995.

COCO CHANEL

(1883–1971) Legendary French fashion designer and businesswoman. The namesake of the Chanel brand, she is the

only fashion designer listed on *Time* magazine's list of the one hundred most influential people of the twentieth century.

Hello Miss Sandy,

I admit to being legendary, but it was a hard fight to get there. Life is always a struggle even when wheels are greased in one's favour.

Interesting the spelling of *favour* in the paragraph above. I kept wanting to change it to the American spelling of favor but I couldn't make myself write it that way. I think there was a little of Coco's prompting involved at that point. Since she also spoke English, perhaps she preferred the English spelling.

I fought for every bit of what I had. I sacrificed, compromised, and sold my soul (in some ways) to fulfill my dreams. Although some may not recognize this, women struggle harder in life to be heard, to be taken seriously, and finally to be respected. We work twice as hard for half the credit men receive.

I don't believe that will ever change but we women know differently. Women have a higher tolerance for physical pain: witness childbirth. We have much more patience: witness how long it takes to reach the top. And, we always have been much wiser: evident in grade averages and the fact we simply live life smarter, so we live longer! Still, only a small percentage of us reach our full potential.

I'm here to tell women that regardless of pettiness, jealousy, and stupid behavior, all women revel in the ultimate success of others [women]. *We all truly support one another. We wear our designs, mimic our "looks," patronize our performances* [on screen—TV and movie— and in theater], *read our books, and adore and copy the finesse others used to climb the social, financial, and corporate ladders.*

In the paragraph that follows, Coco Chanel refers to women as the majority in numbers. In the world although men have a tiny advantage in size across the world, it appears not to be the case in France. By the age of twenty-five, women begin to outnumber men in that country and the numerical difference between men and women increases with age—so she was correct in her assumption. I just looked it up.

We are the majority. We can't give in. We can't quit fighting, for when one sails ahead, twenty others can advance more quickly in her wake.

I hope you love my work and designs [for] *I love everything each of you are doing!!*

With support from here—Coco Chanel

Many centuries earlier but still in France, we jump from the famous to the infamous. When reading the first paragraph of Marie Antoinette's message, I could picture myself in eighteenth century France confronted by some of the decisions to which she refers. They aren't decisions we'd make today but it's easy to draw parallels. Other points in her communication are applicable, regardless of the century in which we find ourselves.

MARIE ANTOINETTE

(1755–1793) The last queen of France prior to the French Revolution, who was selfish and unpopular. Her life ended with an unpleasant death by guillotine.

Hello Sandy,

My name is Marie Antoinette. I suppose I'm a surprise, too. I've come to speak about the confusing role women face and have always faced: to be simple or elegant, to defend our honor or manner by marrying, to have charitable hearts or take for fear of loss later. It's always been an issue, more so for women since men help one another; women seldom do.

I was always alone. I worried about me and put on a mask of who I was each day to protect myself from the realities of the world in which I lived. I suppose people know only the bad about me but let that be a lesson. Words have power, especially when one is on top. A few words can crush the spirit of another, topple governments or ruin one's reputation forever.

Advice—and a great learning from [someone now] *living in love. Pause with a charitable heart and be led to speak from your soul. If a person can do that, it will always ring true to others and be clothed in love, either consciously or subconsciously. Regardless, people will feel it.*

I wish you much luck on your amazing journey, my friend. You have always been a truth-teller, but this is a better time for that gift to blossom since now you are living in love.

Hope we will meet one day. I think highly of you and what you do. Marie A.

Is there any question that Marie Antoinette regretted her comment, "*Let them eat cake*!"? Whether true or not, that sentiment represented how people perceived her, what she did and how she lived—so the phrase immortalized her reputation forever.

Gold Meir came to me twice and her first message is the one that can be applied to all women who search for credibility. Golda, however, had an advantage: she was not a handsome woman but held an extraordinarily powerful position as the only woman prime minister of Israel and the first woman leader in any Middle Eastern country. The world looked up to her.

GOLDA MEIR (1of 2)

(1898–1978) An Israeli stateswoman, politician, teacher and kibbutznik who served as the fourth prime minister of Israel.

Hello beautiful Sandy,

I'm a woman coming to share wisdom from over here, and to reach out to you for help. I'd love to throw my hat in the ring in terms of sharing information that has been impactful to me here, as I reflected on my life and the life of those around me. It's amazing how enlightened we can become with a totally different perspective, and seeing everything through a filter of peace, love, and frankly, bliss.

My name is Golda Meir. I was already an old lady when you were young, so the time in history I lived was slightly different than today. I was resilient, strong, determined, and resolute in the decisions I made. People respected me. I guess I was a pioneer, but I don't think of myself that way in this last life; I think of myself more as a leader who had to step in to get things done.

There was much prejudice in the world then; hidden but existing. Today, it's more open, which is very healthy. When we see it, we can speak up and balance out that judgment with love, not for the person with the prejudice but for the people being persecuted. Does that make sense?

You see, love is always the way to go. It is just which way we direct it. We should have a respect for all life since we are all God's creations. But we are perfectly within our rights to have boundaries and balance what we do that is good with the not-so-good. Evil should be off the table, totally, but you'd be surprised at all the evil that exists. It takes the strong to fight that. I was strong.

The reason I came to you, Sandy, is to remind you of your strength, too. You are a strong woman: strong in determination and focus. You make things happen. You see what needs to be done and you move forward. That is what leaders do. I was not as delicate as you, perhaps because of my appearance, but I was respected. The more beautiful a woman is the less instant respect she receives from men. You have always been different in that way because you are so very smart, people see that quickly and that is when the respect builds.

Of course, now that you're getting a few years on yourself and look more like me (a joke), you'll have all the credibility you can handle. Wisdom, my dear, is the best. Even beats the devil out of smart. Wisdom is the magnificent blend of smart and experienced. Now, you have both.

So, my message is short, and to you. Stay fearless, stay strong, stay determined, and keep up the good fight. Your value to all of us is immeasurable and we not only applaud your work, but we are here to serve you in any way you wish. If you want to include us in speeches or books, it's fine with me and I'll bet it's fine with others. No egos anymore. Or merely take our wisdom and share it as your own; whatever works for the audience.

Meanwhile, we stand ready to be of service. Good job, Sandy, can you imagine, you're just starting?

Your friend and fellow "woman," Golda Meir

This is the message I was a little surprised to receive but also a little excited. I had hoped she'd clear up a few things, but I've learned never to expect a thing from those who come.

NICOLE BROWN SIMPSON

(1959–1994) The ex-wife of former professional American football player O. J. Simpson and the mother of two children. She was killed at her home, along with her friend Ron Goldman, two years after her divorce. Her husband's trial was covered internationally.

Hello my friend,

I feel it is very natural to call you that. Well, I certainly became famous after my death, didn't I? You, like most people, were glued to your televisions not because of concern for me or Ron but by the shock of O.J.'s involvement. A lousy way to become so well-known, but that was my path.

I suppose everyone will want to know: the answer is yes. But the purpose for all that was to be a lasting message to humanity that regardless of race, it's celebrity and money that skews the legal system one way or another. Many people still don't get that.

I think the saddest part is what this put our children through. It's amazing how our minds protect us by adding filters that see only the positive and not letting us see the horrors of reality. One day bits of light will filter in [for them]. But when children have enormous amounts of love in their lives, it's like being wrapped in a blanket , a thick plush blanket, that protects us from reality. My family did that for my darlings.

The other issue that was to eventually surface and that—so, only after numerous books, documentaries, and post analyses like the tipping of the legal scales (abusive violence) is never [about] *jealousy, it's* [about losing] *control, which many still don't get, either! Women are often in the greatest threat when their independence surfaces with or without separation; when a woman steps into her power and the partner no longer has control. They* [the abusers] *panic when reality hits and that's what happened here. O.J. finally realized I was really through and, because he was used to winning his entire life, he couldn't lose—or lose control.*

So, I thought I'd come now, Sandy, to make these two points for the slower learners among you. ☺ Yes, I can still be happy and find joy. My purpose has been completed and now I can rest in the arms of God, with eternal bliss!

Tell everyone I felt little, and it was shock that protected me. It's O.J. who will suffer his remaining life when he becomes weak and vulnerable, in dreams, how his uncontrollable anger shapes his outlook on life and the perception through which he sees the world, and (finally) to be publicly shunned by so many after years of adoration. Painful, I'd say.

Thank you, my new friend, for your work with domestic violence victims and your real understanding of the horrific life many people lead. I stress women because we are the majority and majority of resulting deaths.

You are a bright light, Sandy. The world needs what you are offering. Nicole.

Chapter 4

SOULFUL REGRETS

Every one of us has regrets about something we did or didn't do in our lives. Generally, those feelings of guilt involve isolated situations we can identify and describe. Very few of us have the objectivity and humility to look at the entirety of our lives in an analytical manner. More importantly, most of us haven't lived long enough for a truly accurate reflection of the person we were totally. These souls have.

In the afterlife, objectivity comes naturally as a lifetime is reviewed and reviewed again. It's then a soul begins to see the glaring issues that highlighted their shortcomings. First comes their awareness, then the acknowledgement of that imperfection, and finally owning up to that behavior and taking responsibility. It's the responsibility part that gives those on the other side the incentive to one day attempt to correct the error of their ways and further learn the lessons they still need to learn so the parts of their soul that remains flawed can become refined. Some souls reach these conclusions sooner than others.

The souls who present messages in this chapter seem the most able to articulate powerful critiques of themselves and share their regrets with remarkable candor. It's impossible to read these comments without recognizing how deeply they each dug into their past life on earth to reach the conclusions they did. Such realization wasn't an intellectual exercise, although many express their conclusions simply; each "aha" was a reckoning at the soul level.

These poignant communications help us gain a deeper understanding of people we may have long adored, admired, or judged as being one way, when in fact they were something totally different.

MARILYN MONROE

(1926–1962) American actress and model, she was famous for playing "blonde bombshell" characters and was one of the most popular sex symbols of the 1950's and early 1960's.

My dear Sandy,

Can I be your friend? In my life on earth, I really needed true friends, but I was very insecure. As sexy and as pretty as people believed I was, I just wanted people to see past all that and see me. Isn't that what everyone wants?

Yes, my life was huge, but very superficial. That's all anyone wanted of me, the superficial—so I gave it to them, just to be loved. Real love, however, is what you are trying to teach, and I applaud you for that.

I know we could have been dear friends because you always love people's souls first and worry about everything else after. I hope people listen. I also hope people believe that connecting at the soul level is the most glorious gift of all and now that I'm here, it's the only way I can connect! That's good.

Please, Sandy, encourage people to open their hearts to us, to what we might be trying to say to them, or even to an individual in your own life who was important in some way. We'd love to reach out but it's generally a very futile exercise. Maybe you can help change that.

I did not commit suicide although I was depressed often in my life. I couldn't see a long future for me aging given how my life was structured. Hard to build a skyscraper on a sandy beach. But, still, I would never have intentionally done myself in.

I guess it [my death] *was a gift, anyway. People mourned me, people missed me, and I died young and beautiful. What a tragic way to sum up someone's life. All I ever wanted was soul-based love. I thought I had it a couple times, but my insecurity got in the way.*

Lesson for young women: beauty is fleeting. If you base your self-esteem on that, you'll have a dreadful and lonely life, even if surrounded by men. Cultivate other gifts: be smart, be interesting, be funny. So many talents attract others. You'll find lasting friendships with people who might even look deeper and touch your soul.

Congratulations on "Hi Momma, It's Me," Sandy. A beautiful book and your next and next. I'll be one of your biggest fans. With love, Marilyn

Marilyn Monroe's was a sad commentary about a lonely and troubled life. However, she was right when she said we might have been friends. Some people need more understanding than others and those are the ones I've always adored most.

BING CROSBY

(1903–1977) American singer, comedian, and actor. First multimedia star, he was one of the most popular and influential artists of the twentieth century.

Well, well my Sandy.

You grew up with my voice, didn't you? Sweet Marie always sang with my records. She called me Der Bingle. I'm flattered now to see that.

Marie was my adopted mother and she adored Bing Crosby. I can remember as a little girl, mom playing his records and singing along with them. When he appeared on television, she would be glued to the set. Bing was very handsome and had an incredible voice at the time. She referred to him as "Der Bingle." I believe that began with German fans but quickly spread to many others.

I was a musical celebrity of great magnitude back then. I relished that. I had a big ego and welcomed the acclaim. I was not a good human being, however: unfaithful, driven by greed on several levels—possessions I had were very important to me and I even considered my boys [as] *such. I should have shown my children and the women in my life more love but I'm not sure I knew how.*

Being here brought such insight. Not immediately but eventually. Anyone who would read this today wouldn't remember me now. Perhaps vaguely, by name, so it's perfectly fine to reveal whatever you think would help.

People are mistaken when they put celebrities in some sort of elevated status. Their talent may be admirable, but the people rarely are. Always study their personal lives, their warmth with which they communicate publicly; it's always telling and the generosity they demonstrate.

I was a Catholic, a professional one. Thought it bolstered my image. Even my wife Katherine bolstered my image: young, beautiful—in a wholesome way—and sweet. I was a shallow man, not worthy of the reverence I received and up here, as I look around, I see those that truly deserve such honor. Quiet dutiful servants to mankind, who may be ridiculed or ignored yet they are the ones who deserve undying love and respect.

I'm now much more humble and have grown. I look at your work, Sandy, and this time am anxious to serve. You are a gift to many and one who needs recognition, besides you're sure pretty for your age!! ☺ *You'll receive all of that here. Can't wait to meet you and join the chorus of supporters singing you home. Der Bingle*

DEAN MARTIN

(1917–1995) American singer, actor, and comedian. One of the most handsome and popular and enduring American entertainers of the mid-twentieth century. He was a partner with Jerry Lewis (Martin and Lewis) and later was part of Frank Sinatra's Rat Pack.

Hello there!

Dean Martin here. Boy, talk about celebrating, I was the example of that my entire life. I celebrated an audience. I celebrated friendships. I celebrated a new record. Heck, I celebrated the sunset. Didn't matter. Life was one big party and I made life fun for a lot of people.

When my son died, I got real serious about drinking. Frankly, I must have had a cast iron body because I put so much alcohol into it over the years. Had it really bothered me after, I would have likely toned it down. But we all drank then, you remember.

Alcohol really isn't that great. It just numbs you and releases inhibitions. Yet some of us were uninhibited anyway! WOW! Today people are much smarter about that and that's good.

If I had a message for anyone or a lesson I've learned, I guess it would be not to set yourself on fire just to light up the room. Personality is great but what I was doing to my body and life was destructive and eventually killed me. I really didn't care and was anxious to be near my son again. Now we're all here: Frank [Sinatra], *Sammy* [Davis, Jr], *Joey* [Bishop]— *everybody! Jilly* [Rizzo—restaurateur], *all the people I enjoyed. Even Jerry* [Lewis].

So, the end comes for us all. I just say, what's the rush? Take better care of yourself. You can light up a room with a flashlight and have just as much fun.

Gee, you're doing some work over there. We're all watching. I also notice the room your friend, Carole, has dedicated to me! The power of celebrity, goodness. But I was a charmer. ☺ Am I charming you? Didn't think so. Ha! You're too smart for that.

Good luck, kid. I admire the heck out of you, and you are (a) great looking lady for seventy-six. Keep it up! People can't ignore you when you look that good.

Gotta run, but I'll be around. XXOO Dean

See what I mean about the complete honesty? When we pass to the other side, all the baggage we carried around in this life drops away: the bad habits, the ego, and all the fear-based emotions. We are stripped to our soul so all that remains is the truth of the lives we've led and the love with which we're currently capable. It's from that level of purity that we continue to perfect the beauty of our souls.

JUDY GARLAND

(1922–1969) American actress, singer, vaudevillian, and dancer with a career spanning forty-five years and winning every conceivable award. She's best known for her role in *The Wizard of Oz.*

Hello there, Sandy.

I'm actually honored to be talking to you and I haven't really done any of this before, but I sure welcome the opportunity.

WOW. When I look around so much has changed—not all for the better, I'm afraid. The music is interesting and so unique in some aspects. What we can do with the human voice has expanded dramatically as well. Guess we were more simple (in my day) but star quality is still star quality. Now we see bits of that everywhere.

My life was rough, really. The pills and alcohol blurred the sharp edges and numbed the pain. Try as I might, I had a hard time getting it right. I did love my babies though, but I was even limited in that expression due to the need to put food on the table.

You've had a rough life, too, Sandy but you are strong and have better sense than I did. Be grateful for the talents you were given. I didn't spend enough time in gratitude and see that now. Gratitude is the giant key that unlocks more and more blessings.

Well, honey. I've gotta run. Going to chase a rainbow! Judy

Judy's sign off brought tears to my eyes. I guess that is all I can say about her message. Her closing touched my heart.

KAREN CARPENTER

(1950–1983) American singer with a group called "The Carpenters," which included her brother. She died as a result of her anorexia.

Hi Sandy.

So many of us want to talk to you because we have something to say, either about our lives and the lessons we learned or advice we wish to give others, based on those same lessons. I sure am here for that reason.

I was a poster girl for anorexia. I suffered with this most of my adult life and, of course, my life ended way too soon. When I sang, the music came directly from my soul; if the truth be told, there wasn't much fat or muscle to muffle the sound. A thin wall between my voice and the listeners. I loved what I did, and my brother was such a talented arranger and partner. We were quite a pair but, in the end, the disease won out.

I've reviewed my life and see where I went wrong. Where I failed to surrender to God instead of trying to control a life that was spinning out of control. God would have protected me, I would have felt less stress, and I could have continued with a life that touched the hearts of so many. It never works to try to control anything, you know. We really have no control, and in the end, the efforts to control wrap around us like a giant python, eventually choking the life from us. A terrible way to die.

Anorexia isn't the only disease caused by over-controlling oneself, or others. Parkinson's disease and so many others [too].

Control is evil because it is based out of fear: fear of finding freedom, finding the answers, being able to handle one's life, and so the only thing we are able to control is ourselves. In my case, it was over-controlled. It distorted my perspective on my body, on what I needed, and [on] what was good for me. I was a foolish young woman.

I'll be back soon because I know I can help people in many ways because of what I have learned about love and God and life. Talking to you is just the start.

Sandy, I'm not sure if I made sense at all. I know you believe some of this, which is why I was eager to reach out. Our energy seemed compatible. Plus, I think you related to my music and would sing along with me. That's nice, too.

I'm happy I met you and I thank you for giving me a start at helping others. In this last life, I couldn't even help myself. So, from this point on, everything is up.

With love and in an energetic harmony, I remain, Karen Carpenter

Reading these messages will hopefully provide a few pointers to those of you in the process of self-reflection or merely thinking about tackling that subject. The talents needed to do so are total objectivity, honesty, and humility. The benefit of self-reflection is monumental in the scheme of things, with the eventual goals being to become less judgmental of others, more forgiving of ourselves and others, and more compassionate to all.

Robert Stack was one of the people, who when he showed-up, I questioned what he could possibly contribute. He wasn't particularly famous and would probably not rank on anyone's top five list of people they'd love to meet. Yet, every soul who came astounded me with the messages they wanted to share, and Robert Stack was the perfect example of someone who delivered a missive from which so many of us could learn. I thought he was amazing.

ROBERT STACK

(1919–2003) American actor and television host, he appeared in over forty feature films, starred in the ABC-TV series *The Untouchables* and hosted/narrated *Unsolved Mysteries*. He won an Emmy Award and was nominated for an Academy Award.

Hi Sandy,

Isn't this wonderful, what you are doing and making available to us? Golly, I can hardly believe it. If I was still an earthling, I'm not sure I'd buy into any of this, but I can see clearly from here what a benefit this connecting can be. And it's fun for someone like me who has never experienced anything quite like this.

So, I guess I'm supposed to spout poetic about something! Well, I can say that I wasn't a perfect man and didn't have a perfect life; I'd guess I'd fall right in the middle of not too bad and not too good—not the extreme on either side. I don't think my calling was to do much more than experience life, entertain a few people (with my craft) and try to be a decent husband and parent. I tried.

Guess if I had any regrets, it may be that I didn't step up for the big risks or take on the big challenges. I played it safe much of my life. That was fine but a little boring [now] *in retrospect when I look around here and pay attention to the people who are coming to you who really stepped-it-up in their lives. Big ideas, big challenges, and big wins. I was pretty average, I guess, but I'm sure most people who will read this will say, "Oh, for goodness' sake, he was a movie and TV star. That's something!" They'd be right in terms of picking a career, but not in terms of what I did within the confines of the career I chose.*

I'd say, if I had advice for anyone, I'd tell them to take risk. Try it. If you fail, nobody really knows or cares in the scheme of things. But if you succeed, you could really make a huge difference for others either through your efforts or the fruits from your labors—the people you hire, the philanthropy that becomes possible, or the ultimate message of that work. Stick your neck out.

If I lived that particular life all over again, I'd push myself in my craft. I'd work harder and stretch in more challenging roles. I'd love to see what my limits would have been. I actually think I was a pretty good actor, but I'd have liked to have been a fine one!

Thank you, Sandy, for this. Gee, I feel better just saying all of this to someone. Maybe this experience will provide a focus for my next life... something to work toward. God gave us all these magnificent bodies with all the talents and capabilities we rarely use. Maybe we honor God by trying to use some of those gifts that are just lying dormant.

See? I may think about that one as a goal when I return again. Boy, this connecting is something. I'd say you stretched on this deal, Sandy. You're a good example for us all.

With much admiration, Robert Stack

PRINCE

(1958–2016) American singer, songwriter, multi-instrumentalist, record producer, dancer, actor, and director. Regarded as one of the greatest musicians of his generation, he embraced gender fluidity.

Hi Miss Sandy –

I don't think you were a big fan of mine or if, for that matter, would even know a song of mine if it appeared on the radio. That's OK. You were open to us all and we all truly appreciate that.

Now that we've connected, I'd be curious to see if you can relate to any of my music. I was flamboyant. Black gay men were not embraced by Blacks. If you can remember Johnny Mathis hid his identity for decades and decades. He wasn't too popular with Blacks anyway.

I was more flashy, like Rod Stewart and Mick Jagger. That was acceptable. Then the rock culture embraced all the androgynous types like Queen, Elton John. And it didn't matter, we were entertainers, and it wasn't the person that kept fans, it was our music.

I always felt like an imposter in life. I donned my garments and became who I presented to fans and lost myself along the way. Not sure I ever really knew who I was. Here I see the real me. The soul is all that survives and that was the true me. Beautiful, lovely, a little needy but kind. I'll get this right next time around. I'll even refine my talent. It's much more powerful when executed at the soul level. I'll bet my music would change (however) the mechanics and musicality remain good, but the interpretation is what touches people's hearts, not minds. Nor with a goal merely being to move feet.

I was still pretty good (smile),but have a lot of work to do. A stupid ending to a life not yet fully blossomed. Most sincerely, Sandy, Prince

After Prince's message, I did a little research because I was curious about him. I thought it was surprising that no one referred to him as gay and he didn't seem to have a "coming out" moment. He was married twice but was clearly androgynous in his appearance and the way he performed. His inference about being gay stuck with me and I thought if that was truly the case, I could see why he'd feel like an imposter while he was alive. If he meant something else it was disturbing. How sad that one's life can either be so busy or filled with so many distractions that there's no time for contemplating and self-reflection. Equally tragic, if at the time, a person could be so intimidated by society that they would hide their real self.

Chapter 5

MORE INSIGHTS ON CONNECTING ACROSS DIMENSIONS

It's impossible to learn all there is to learn about the prospect of connecting with souls on the other side. The reason for this difficulty is how complex the process is. Besides the obvious benefits those of us still living receive, the benefits to the souls over there are more subtle, individualized, therefore, more complicated. Paul Harvey and Lee Iacocca, in Chapter 1, provided a wonderful summary in overview form and expressed the value of cross-dimensional connecting with great clarity. Still, others who came to me wanted to be included on this topic, too, each offering additional justification here and there. That's why this chapter was added. Some of the following souls contributed very little but some said a lot.

Spencer Tracy was one of the first of the additional group to offer his opinion. Although it took me a while to figure out who he was, I eventually got it. I was quite young when Spencer Tracy reached his peak in the movies, so it seems I was only aware of him during his last ten years on earth. I recognized his name, could picture his face, and remembered his memorable romance with Katherine Hepburn, but for the life of me couldn't name one movie in which he appeared. He was patient with my ignorance.

SPENCER TRACY

(1900–1967) Leading man in Hollywood's Golden Age, receiving nine nominations and two Oscars. Although still legally married, he had a long-term love affair with actress Katherine Hepburn.

Hello, Miss Sandy,

I know this is a surprise. I'm another person you've never heard from before, but I couldn't resist contacting you. I can see why you are typing this one. Hand tired, huh? Well, that son of yours is an amazing fellow, too

Spencer Tracy's reference to how tired my hand had become made me smile since taking dictation for multiple souls when they show up in a single day makes my head ache and my hand tired. Although I always prefer handwriting, which feels more intimate to me, I'm often forced to type what I hear on the computer. This was one such case. Tracy continued:

My name is Spencer Tracy. I know you are aware of who I am because I think you have watched some of my movies. I came to show my respect for the work you are doing. I had wanted to reach out so badly, when I died, to a couple people in my life and they were totally unable to receive anything from me. It would have helped my healing immensely but most importantly, helped my soul to recover from the terrible guilt I felt.

Your book will help educate people. It will help people, at least, open to the possibility. And what happened with me is while I was reliving all the pain I caused (that was a lengthy process) and I think you know to whom I'm referring: my wife and family, specifically…

I'm sorry to interject once more but sometimes a comment made by a soul is not explained enough for everyone to understand it. Spencer

Tracy's comment about having regrets about the pain he caused his family was just such a case.

Although never divorced because of their Catholic religion, Spencer Tracy and his wife simply separated and for twenty-six years his family had to bear witness to the ongoing and very public love affair he had with Katherine Hepburn, another star from that era. It must have been horrible for his wife to watch as Tracy and Hepburn's extraordinary love affair played out in every tabloid imaginable.

Spencer Tracy felt that pain, too, since on the other side souls feel the anguish they cause others in magnified form. Although it appears he tried to reach out to his wife to tell her how sorry he was, his attempts were futile.

In this next paragraph, Spencer continues by explaining how once souls are aware of the wrongs they caused, the issue becomes how to correct the error of their ways since there is really no mechanism to execute that last element of making amends in Heaven.

> *...[over here] I was isolated and merely cleansing. Not cleansing and learning at the same time. It is an easier process to see what you have done and then connect and make amends at the same time; that process is an experiential exercise in growth. Instead, over here, we almost all have to do it one thing at a time, each in isolation. Not nearly as powerful. Then, when my family got here, the process becomes much different: soul to soul since there is no earth reference, so no* [soul] *growth* [occurs] *from those rekindled relationships.*

Although souls do reconnect in the afterlife, there is no earth reference once souls meet: just familiarity, love and basic energy. They don't communicate the same way as they did on earth, and they don't bring with those Heavenly energy exchanges any memory of the details of their immediate lives on earth. The connection over there is more about pure love and familiarity, but no details. So, there is no way to correct past wrongs without returning in another life to do so in some other circumstance.

Now, do you see how valuable your work is? Please, with your many interviews and times to share, perhaps speeches, try to explain this phenomenon to others so they grasp the power of us connecting across the veil, as many people like to refer to this. I personally like dimensions, the phrase you use, because it is more complex than a simple piece of sheer fabric.

Sandy, I hope it is OK that I reached out to you. I realize I am a real odd connection, not a glamour boy that people would be flattered hearing from like the "in a prior life I was once Cleopatra" stories. You know how everyone likes the glamorous and famous. Well, I guess I was well-known but surely not glamorous. I was a simple sort, did love my craft, and had real, deep relationships while on earth. Probably not the normal Hollywood type. ☺

When I look at you and your life, I am so impressed. There you are—a nobody, really—from a tiny town in the Midwest, adopted and no real formal education, but look at what you have accomplished in your life: spurred the growth of companies, reached out to communicate for women in domestic violence, were an amazing role model for healing, aged beautifully, and helped grow nonprofits. It is over and over and over. And now you are helping us.

Please know how deeply we appreciate who you are and what you are doing. You have our love and support and respect. Thanks for taking time to hear me and I hope I said something that will be meaningful to your work. It is with great admiration that I reached out to you.

Your humble servant, up here or over here. HA! And, now your friend, Spencer

Mickey Mantle's message contained two distinct topics, so I felt compelled to feature him in two different chapters. Here, I've lifted only the paragraphs that apply to this subject from the second half. You'll read the first half from Mickey later.

MICKEY MANTLE (2 of 2)

(1931–1995) This major league baseball great played his entire career for the New York Yankees as a center fielder, right fielder, and first baseman. He was legendary.

Now that I've been submerged in the bliss that exists up here and have had enough time for a slow-learner like me to figure this all out—ha, I want to give back. Returning [to another life] to do this work is more challenging because some of my own context from the lessons are lost; so, I'm afraid, my passion wouldn't be as great. No memory of previous lives or lessons, you know.

God set up a great system for our individual refinement, but I think he wanted someone like you to open a few more doors to the public about how both of our dimensions (you there and us here) can continue our soul growth in an accelerated manner. It's time for that now. And you drew the short straw. HA!

"Batter Up!" You're up now my new friend, and I know your efforts will hit it out of the park, over and over. Blessings coming from another new friend, and admirer (always liked blondes)!!! ☺
Mickey

This next surprise visitor was a person dear to my heart because of the work she did. I had met Elisabeth Kübler-Ross briefly while she was alive, and we had mutual friends in common whom she mentioned earlier in her message to me. Also, she thanked me for including her in the book prior and heaped on quite a bit of praise, which I thought was needlessly gratuitous, so I chose not to include Elisabeth's entire message. The reason Elisabeth Kübler-Ross appears in this chapter is that this woman opened the door to the study of death and dying. Yet, as even she admits, her work was just the beginning.

ELISABETH KÜBLER-ROSS

(1926–2004) A Swiss-American psychiatrist, a pioneer in near-death studies, and author of the internationally bestselling book *On Death and Dying*

Hello, Sandy.

Now, let me tell you a bit about here. I had a vague idea but my limited perspective prior to passing was exactly that. Very limited. This is the most idyllic, magnificent environment anyone could imagine. The richness and depth are astounding. No subtleties here at all— gloriousness at its most grand. I'm honored to be in the presence of so many glowing spirits, many of whom I instantly recognized by feeling but also by love for those I cared about in my lifetime.

Just wait, sister, until you arrive. Lots of souls to welcome you. We are all so grateful for your work. Why? Not because it benefits the world. Many do that. Not because it benefits you. Everybody tries for that. But, instead of using us for some other good purpose, your work actually benefits us! Imagine! Nobody does that.

You were given a real job toward the end of your life, dear one. This is a biggie. Special? I guess so. So, I wanted you to know that you have my support and all of our love. It's flooding your way.

Signing off now. If you ever meet my son, give him a hug. He's a good one.

Much love—my new friend, Elisabeth

Following is the second of Golda Meir's communications with me, each coming within a few weeks of the other. She was particularly excited about the concept of this book.

GOLDA MEIR (2 of 2)

My dear Sandy,

Thank you for hearing me, once again. I like the idea for your new book. By reaching out to help others we help balance the wrongs in our past life. It is remarkably healing for us. So, we're doing our part to reach out to one who understands and is the perfect communication vehicle—you! Then you have the difficult part, spreading the word to the masses, so we can actually make a difference from here.

The connectedness is so very valuable since it shortens the number of times we must return in total ignorance, and spend years becoming aware, refining our spirit, and making amends thru karma-based relations. Your work short cuts all of that. Do you realize how huge this is?

Someone should pay you to write so you needn't spend countless hours toiling in some unrelated job. You are our hero, Sandy. I send you my strength and my love. We are all here cheering you on!

With sincere fondness, forever, Golda

CHRISTA McAULIFFE

(1948–1986) American teacher and astronaut who was one of seven crew members killed in the Space Shuttle Challenger disaster.

Dearest Sandy,

I'm here to bring greetings from the entire space mission crew. We never got to say goodbye to so many we loved and left behind. That was the most difficult thing about leaving so you can imagine how important your work is to us.

Other mediums respond to the one person in front of them, allowing one or two [spirits] *to reach them. Other celebrity types* [mediums] *reach only those in their audience with* [messages *from] their family or loved ones. You, on the other hand, let us speak to whomever in the world wants to hear; hopefully some we knew. If not, then you educate the ones you reach that all this is possible.*

You realize I was an educator, too, so we are kindred spirits, of sorts. I loved dearly everyone in my life—my family and friends. I was focused and my career elevated me some. It's funny how people respond to those who are different by virtue of their achievements. That's sad. People's hearts and souls are still the same, they are just wearing a professional uniform of some kind over their same old body!!

Thank you so much for this grand opportunity. Please don't let our deaths dissuade anyone from pursuing the space program. It's Heaven, indeed! Christa

Christa summed it all up with her first paragraph. This was a way for her to say goodbye since her life ended so abruptly. Can you imagine how that must be true for so many who experience a very unexpected death from a tragic accident or some sort of a disaster? It's sad when we're taken quickly and don't have adequate time to communicate with those we love. Yes, reconnecting has its purposes.

This last participant didn't really talk about the benefits of connecting but rather discussed the benefits of expanding one's perspective to include possibilities beyond the "known." Harry Houdini was mysterious, magical, and made us believe that some people have special gifts; with his explanation he was correct in one way and incorrect in another.

Some people do have special gifts since it's their unusual combination or degree of capability that allows them to standout. Others, however, may seem unique in what they do but have the very same gifts you have, the difference being they allow themselves to experience those gifts. Houdini used me as an example of that.

This closing message was a hybrid of sorts so that's why it ended up here. I think it's appropriate and I hope his thoughts will leave you even more curious.

HOUDINI

(1874–1926) Harry Houdini was a Hungarian-born American escape artist, illusionist, stunt performer, and "mysteriarch," noted for his escape acts.

Hi Sandy, I'm Harry Houdini, at least that was my stage name.

Well, you have a few gifts, don't you? I had a few also: physical ones that let my body contort a bit, intuitive ones that helped me know to do first, second and so forth, and creative gifts to [allow me to] *come up with stunts and escape tricks that shocked the world. I'm reluctant to use the word trick because one needed all my gifts to live the life I did.*

My purpose [in life] *was similar to yours: to challenge man with these feats, to make them believe in possibilities and see potential in themselves they may not have recognized. "If he can do this, maybe I can do something challenging and difficult in my own life." I wanted people to be amazed but also inspired, not unlike you. You stun folks with what you are able to deliver but you're so normal otherwise that people can maybe believe in their own exceptionalism.*

I call people to accept the challenge of believing there may still be much in the world and in life they don't understand. Be open to such mysteries and always trust that God will deliver what's right for you.

Thank you, colleague. I'm in your debt for finally figuring out I was there and for inclusion in this wonderful book. Harry H.

Chapter 6

THE IMPORTANCE OF HUMOR

If it's good enough for the Dalai Lama, it's good enough for me. Laughter, that is. Did you ever notice how happy the Dalai Lama always seems to be? Even as an admired spiritual leader, he smiles frequently and laughs a lot, which are qualities that simply delight me. Through this example alone, how can anyone ignore the importance of appreciating humor?

It's the funnyman and woman that I believe deserves more credit than they get. The humorists, comedic actors, and standup comics possess a gift for making us laugh, and to do so requires them to pay keen attention to the human beings around them. It's that honed human perspective that also gives them an edge with any very complex dramatic role they're offered. If a person understands what makes people tick, they'll see the funny as well as the tragic.

As examples of this point, let's take a look at a few Oscar winning performances from unexpected performers: Red Buttons (*Sayonara*); Art Carney (*Harry and Tonto*) and those receiving not only an Oscar but also other Oscar nominations: Robin Williams (*Good Will Hunting* as well as receiving three other Oscar nominations); Alan Arkin (*Argo* and *Little Miss Sunshine*, plus two other Oscar nominations); Whoopie Goldberg (*Ghost* and one other nomination); and Walter Matthau (*The Fortune Cookie* and two other nominations).

Those who were nominated for Oscars, by giving amazing performances in drama: Woody Harrelson (*The People vs. Larry Flynt*, *The Messenger* and *Three Billboards Outside Ebbing, Missouri*); Bette Midler

(*The Rose*); Jackie Gleason (*The Hustler*); Dan Aykroyd (*Driving Miss Daisy*); Lily Tomlin (*Nashville*); Bill Murray (*Lost in Translation*); Steve Carell (*Foxcatcher*); Melissa McCarthy (*Can You Ever Forgive Me?*); Mary Tyler Moore (*Ordinary People);* and Eddie Murphy (*Dreamgirls*).

Although they weren't Oscar winners or nominees, we also shouldn't overlook Sarah Silverman (*I Smile Back*) and Adam Sandler (*Uncut Gems)* and probably dozens more I've overlooked. I think you get the point.

Finally, comedians also make fine directors: Carl Reiner (*Skokie, Ocean's Eleven*) and Mike Nichols (*Who's Afraid of Virginia Woolf, The Graduate, Catch-22, Carnal Knowledge, Silkwood, The Birdcage, Primary Colors,* and *Charlie Wilson's War*). Again, when you can touch the funny bone it's not that far of a stretch to touch the heart.

So, this chapter is devoted to those who made us smile, giggle, and laugh out loud with their amazing perspective on mankind. Don't be surprised if you find flashes of brilliance and profound thought in the messages that follow.

JACK LEMMON

(1925–2001) American actor and musician who was a celebrated virtuoso in both comedy and drama having been nominated for the Academy Award eight times, winning twice.

Hi Sandy,

I am a happy soul. Some are not. I had a complicated life, as we all do, but it was easy for me to be light of heart with many roles because that's how I truly was.

Some of my finer moments on film were characters with much more depth because I was that as well. We all have many facets to who we are. My dominant role in this last life was lighter.

I wonder if people will understand the point, I just made. The lightness and darkness of our beings. It's easy to succumb to the latter through drugs, alcohol, isolation, repressing anger, and refusing to try to see another's point of view. I think the latter point is the key, for if we cannot imagine the flip side of where we are at the moment, it's impossible to live with gratitude, or have compassion, or grow in faith.

I'll explain all three, if I may. If you are only eating a chicken sandwich for dinner from leftover chicken with mayonnaise, instead of longing for a steak, imagine if you only had one heel of bread left in your fridge and nothing more. How you'd nibble at it to stretch the sensation of its taste. Then, realize what you're eating (the chicken sandwich) with a grateful heart. If you can imagine the emotion and feelings around the alternative, you'll appreciate more of what you have.

It's the same with compassion. When you see a lost or confused soul, imagine their pain and fear and reach out to them with a helping hand: a referral, a patient ear, or a word of support. You have much to give but to do so, you must take time to see the pain others endure.

In terms of faith, whatever you desire most in life, imagine the complete antithesis of having it. Good health? Imagine your life bound to a deathbed for months or years. How would you find joy for yourself [with that existence]*? Look out the window at the beauty of nature, having entertainment on a TV nearby to make you smile and what you could do to lift the spirits of your family, caregivers, and friends. When you accept this could be your life and try to break free of those bonds of fear surrounding the "worst possible scenario," it is easier to relax and open to receive the blessings of God.*

Faith is knowing that whatever God gives you, you will handle it. And, knowing He can and will bring you even more blessings than exist now. Only when fear is removed can you have the unbridled future He promises. And your faith in that future.

That is how I approached my craft and my life. My perspectives could change, and I believe that made me an actor of more depth than many knew.

You are a gift, Sandy. Thank you for opening your mind and heart to us. Jack Lemmon

ERMA BOMBECK

(1927–1996) American humorist who published fifteen bestselling books and had a syndicated newspaper humor column from 1965–1996 describing suburban home life.

Sandy, dear.

You'd never believe it, but humor is alive in Heaven. So many souls are happy, even joyful. The best audience ever.

What a life I had. You know the magic of having a good sense of humor is immeasurable. When a person can see a spark of humor in a tragic event, minimize pain with a good laugh, or use a little sarcasm to make a point lightly, that gift, I think, makes life bearable.

I always saw how to turn the common into the very funny. I had the wit of a very stern but loving mother. I surprised many with what came out of my mouth, and I made life much more fun for some. Not as funny (here) as I used to be but the raw material here isn't as rich. Can't do much with constant bliss, unconditional love everywhere, and peace that permeates all! So, I may disappoint but people can always read my old books and perhaps that will help enrich the family I have remaining. ☺

Tell Rita Davenport "Hi." [She was] *a good friend and natural talent. Wish I'd have had that accent—then I'd have been perfect!*

The last paragraph of Erma's message I included in the final chapter, titled *Irresistible Invitations*, since she joins other souls who invite you to connect with them, whenever you wish. I believe by the time you finish this book, you might be willing to talk to one or two of these extraordinary souls, if the mood strikes you. They may not answer back, but they absolutely will be listening.

By the way, Rita Davenport, who is mentioned one other time in this book, came from the South decades ago but retained her accent, which is charming. As an award-winning keynote speaker, humorist, and author, her style of delivery allows her to say almost anything without the edge or sarcasm. Rita is simply a delight.

LUCILLE BALL

(1911–1989) American actress and television comedian icon. Star of I Love Lucy, *The Lucy Show*, Here's Lucy, and the *Lucy-Desi Comedy Hour*, she was the first female head of a major Hollywood studio, Desilu Productions, which she owned.

Hi there, Sandy.

What a kick this is! I notice you watched Little Lucie, or grown Lucie, on TV yesterday in a rerun and that's what drew my attention to you. Amazing how that energy thing works! HA!

Lucy was referring to her daughter, Lucie Désirée Arnaz, an actress, singer, and producer. Lucille Ball and Desi Arnaz also had a son, Desi Arnaz Jr. (Desiderio Alberto Arnaz IV), also an actor and musician. Interesting names, aren't they?

I guess I'm here to talk about the power of humor, which was my whole life—at least on the screen. Desi was the genius, and he spotted that spark in me going on to produce our remarkable series.

Do you know how wonderful it is to make people laugh and bring joy into their lives? Over and over people watched the same episodes and it didn't matter. Funny is funny! And I was. Pretty enough to not be a clown but uninhibited enough to do whatever I had to do to make a scene work. It just came natural to me.

Still, my personal life wasn't as funny. There's balance you know, Sandy, tradeoffs in every life. Nothing ever flows 100 percent in one direction. That's why believing in something or someone greater than ourselves is the life raft that steadies us when the waves hit.

Personally, I seem to have lived on the ocean during storm season, but no one knew. Demon alcohol.

Lucille Ball's reference to demon alcohol was not about her own life, but about her husband, Desi's. Desi Arnaz's alcoholism led to many other vices including womanizing and gambling. Although the couple divorced in 1960 and both went on to remarry, they still loved each other for their entire lives.

But here God's world is glorious, and I feel chuckles around me, light-hearted spirits, and robustly happy, energetic souls everywhere. Somebody must be playing I Love Lucy reruns on my energy field.

I'm being silly, but I just want to remind everyone to find their safe space in humor: a friend who makes you laugh, experiences that are fun, or programs to watch that lighten your spirit.

I was proud to be part of that necessary world for balance and healthy survival. Thank you for letting me visit. It's been a "Ball"—Lucille

The biggest shock in this chapter was a visit from the broadcast journalist and columnist, and celebrity named Cokie Roberts. She was always a serious reporter all the years that I watched her on television, so with this message she brought something much different to the table.

COKIE ROBERTS

(1943–2019) American journalist and bestselling author. She was a political reporter and analyst for National Public Radio and ABC News.

Hi Sandy,

I'm so happy I could join you. It's refreshing for anyone to seek my opinion anymore. ☺, I'm not unhappy as how could anyone be unhappy in this glorious place with Divinity all around me and every dear soul in my life who passed before me—and a few who have come since —nearby. Heaven is magnificent and there are no complaints. It is just nice that I can reach out and perhaps do some good.

You might be surprised at what I want to talk about to your readers. It is more about life than about news or about the state of politics or even society. It is the simple pleasures of life that I believe most people ignore. I know I did.

What I miss most is laughter. Hearing and reveling in it. A funny event, a good story, a hilarious movie, or whatever. Laugher keeps us young and keeps us healthy. See, you didn't think you'd hear that from me, did you?

Of course, we do feel the energy of joy up here and can recognize those who seem to radiate in that state—the vibration is different, and they actually lift those around them with their frequency. But most are more tranquil beings. I guess that is the same in real life. Most people dutifully drudge through the day, executing their chores and performing tasks. Then, evening comes where some enjoy family and others enjoy a drink, or camaraderie with friends and a drink. HA!

Looking down at humanity today, I see a sense of humor missing. It's a void. Even with late-night television, that used to be hilarious because nothing was sacred: no person, no idea, no political party. Today, everyone is on guard and on guard against each other; dreadful state of affairs.

So, I say, bring back the funny bone. Become reacquainted with our anatomy and see what you've been missing. That funny bone is hidden in there somewhere—look for it, find it, and enjoy it once again.

I'll leave you with a smile, Sandy, and sincere thanks for this opportunity to share my opinion with others. This new book will be a blessing. Cokie

Joan Rivers was known for how she skewered highly visible individuals. Her husband, Edgar Rosenberg committed suicide in 1987. He was Joan's manager and husband of twenty-two years. So, you see, no life is all laughs.

JOAN RIVERS

(1933–2014) An American comedian, actress, writer, producer, and television host. Noted for her acerbic wit especially directed toward celebrities and politicians. She was the first woman to host a late-night television show, from 1989–1993.

Hello, my dear.

I couldn't let you write the chapter on humor in your book without including me. My ego didn't quite disappear. That's a joke. Actually, I did notice when Phyllis and Lucille came to you, and I guess I just didn't move fast enough. It's easy to be distracted over here… the harp music.

Well, I was surprised to arrive and find people I never would have thought would wind up in this destination. Frankly, I wasn't too certain about myself—and even Edgar since he had such a tragic end. Yet here we both are! Still in love, well, love is the only option in this place.

God is certainly grand and even though my sarcasm is still alive and well, I know when to relax a bit and give time for people to realize it's all in fun. I'm not as caustic as I once was.

My life was quite a success. I lived a lavish lifestyle, and my places looked a little like Mar-a-Lago, but I loved it, so I did it. And I'm not embarrassed to say that I deserved every bit of my success. I worked my butt off.

If I could leave people today with one important thought, it's how critical the work ethic is. You can't get to the other side of the lake in a rowboat if you refuse to pick up the oars. Everything takes effort and once you get used to it, it just becomes a way of life. Your life expands to give you enough time to sleep and eat and have fun. But it is the energy around work that should be the driver in everyone's life. Particularly important that you enjoy what you've chosen and if you're ambivalent about whether you love it or not, try to see the good in it. Appreciate the opportunity and pretty soon, it won't be bad at all.

Can you imagine how difficult it is for comedians who might have a gift but are terrified to get on stage? How do you enjoy and love what you do, if you are scared to death (to do it)? Well, we learn to do it and you can too. Push the fear of choosing the wrong career, making a mistake, or completely failing out of your mind. Go for it.

And, regardless of the career you choose or the work that eats up your days, find humor in all of it. If you keep a light heart and stop for a minute with open eyes, darned near everything is funny.

Here I am, still speaking up and once in a while even God chuckles. If He can have a sense of humor, you can, too. Oh, I guess that was two messages! Joan Rivers

PHYLLIS DILLER

(1917–2012) American stand-up comedian, actress, and author known for her eccentric stage persona and self-deprecating humor.

Hey—

Well, I went here and not where many would have guessed. I still see life through a lens of humor, but the sharp edges of sarcasm have left. Amazing how most comedians approach their humor through a life of emotional pain born from rejection, indifference, or even abuse. We fight back by being who we were afraid to be in real life.

I'm not making this more deep than it is, but stand-up comedy is extraordinarily tough. Some, though, have a natural gift of timing, a uniqueness to their style and something that makes people remember them. The best comedians take from life. Vulgar language is a trick to shock and fill time when the material is weak.

People laugh when they're uncomfortable, not because the material is funny but because they are nervous about it. You see nervous laughter all the time when Uncle Charlie belches at the table, little Johnny farts, or two kids are caught making out on the porch. Of course, today, innocence is somewhat lost so instead of innocent, nervous laughter we find belligerence, defiance, and anger as substitutes.

We've lost our sense of humor, or rather the innocent core in us that could keep humor alive. I'm glad I left before all of this was ushered in. I was irreverent and extreme, but my material was based on truth, truth 80 percent of the people saw. Today, lies qualify, vicious attacks are encouraged, and nibbling around the edges of this life experience is lost to those who go for the jugular with a dagger.

Sandy, I admire you. Your sense of humor is there but it's your love that shines through. Life can't be taken that seriously. It's over in a flash and then we all face the pain and reality of how we treated others! Eternity doing that number isn't worth a few minutes on the stage of life hating our fellow man.

I leave you with a parting shot of my hair, cigarette holder, and wrinkled face! Boy, I was a beauty—and didn't care! People loved me and I loved them back. Now, I'm here with Fang and we both send our love to you.

Keep it up, Phyllis

For those of you who may not have remembered the extraordinary Phyllis Diller, Fang was how she referred to her husband. I giggled a bit typing his name and I can still hear her cackling laugh. Phyllis was amazing.

We end with Charlie Chaplin. With Charlie Chaplin, no words are needed.

CHARLIE CHAPLIN

(1889–1977) English comic actor, filmmaker, and composer who rose to fame during silent films and became a worldwide icon through is screen persona, "The Tramp."

Dearest Sandy,

I'll bet I'm an unusual voice for you to hear from since my strongest communications skills were using no words at all. It's funny, really, everything started out so naturally, expressing one character's emotions, and look what happened? People fell in love with The Tramp.

Words may have power, but they lose something if spoken by a person with no soul or the wrong soul. Emotion, however, can be conveyed with a single tear, heaving shoulders (sorrow) or terror: eyes wide, shock on the face and hands (palms) out to protect the shoulders and face. Simple gestures yet powerful messages.

Babies understand all of that; it's in our wiring. They respond in kind to big smiles, look quizzically at surprise or fear, and although they mirror joy, they don't "get" the negative stuff.

We are all wired for bliss and joy, our natural state. It is this world we inhabit periodically that corrupts the purity of the soul.

Hug others, smile more often, lean in when others speak. You will connect and bond at a deeper level.

Spread the word, Sandy. You and your work are blessed, my friend. In love and joy, Charlie Chaplin

Chapter 7

ADVICE FOR EVERYONE

Souls on the other side have a unique perspective on the lives they just led. They're also very clear on what behaviors, beliefs or feelings drove their lives or could have been modified to make their lives easier and more satisfying. Can you imagine how blessed we are to vicariously experience that insight and perhaps gain from their newly acquired wisdom? Perhaps some of the issues they faced or challenges they ducked will be helpful for us. That's why I was thrilled to compile this chapter to see if any offered something from which we all might benefit.

You'll also notice a few of the souls mention a link of some type they had with me. I always enjoy hearing those flashes of familiarity but never expect them. It appears those insights come from my energy field where there is a signal of sorts to indicate something we might have in common. Mama Cass, for example, mentioned my enthusiastic sing-along to one of her songs whenever I hear it. She's right, as embarrassing as that might be. She's one of many who force me to tell a few personal stories or explain the context.

MAMA CASS ELLIOT

(1941 –1974) American singer best known for being part of The Mamas and The Papas. She released five solo albums and was posthumously inducted into the Rock and Roll Hall of Fame.

Hey, my friend.

Wanna sing along with me? I think we have the same range. How about "Dream a Little Dream [of Me]?" Yes, I can pick up parallel interests or common experiences in your energy field. Neat, huh? Never got that with drugs! Boy, were some of us stupid about that (drugs). We could have had as much fun with a few beers and lived longer.

I loved our music. We had a sound and were unique. It was my life, and I wasn't the type of person, nor did I have the physical gifts, to make a life doing much else; and I was blessed with a decent voice and the best musical encounters and friendships—ever.

I mentioned the dream song because that's the one you always sing with me!

I have no great message other than to caution about thinking drugs will enhance a person's life. That's BS. It shortens it, almost always. [Instead] *you can find what you're searching for by looking up (or over. HA!) and within. No need to become some monk. Just let Sandy open a couple doors for you and reveal the possibilities!*

Who knows? We might run into each other.

Bye for now, sister! Cass

KENNY ROGERS

(1938–2020) American singer and songwriter elected to the Country Music Hall of Fame in 2013. He charted more than four hundred and twenty hit singles across various genres.

Hello there, young lady.

Kenny Rogers here. I'm not a great philosopher nor do I have brilliant insight on any topic to share other than to remind everyone how simple life really is.

Love those around you. Cherish relationships you have. Be trustworthy and helpful but most importantly remember every person you meet is just as fragile inside as you are. So always be kind.

I was blessed with a wonderful career, which filled my life with music, my passion, and joy. Music made people happy, soothed souls, stirred memories, and created new ones. How blessed I was to be part of that world.

I guess if I could share any one thing that I learned was that life on earth goes by in a heartbeat. It's much too short, if you're loving it, and much too short to repair the damage you've done or to heal completely if you were wounded by this life experience. There is never enough time. So, treasure every moment and every experience.

I almost quoted from "The Gambler" but nobody would believe I'd be that corny (yet I almost was!).

Thank you, Sandy, for this and for the venue you're providing for us.

We all love you, Kenny

For those who might not know, "The Gambler" was one of Kenny Rogers' most famous songs. Probably the most noticeable message in that song was repeated over and over in the chorus:

You've got to know when to hold 'em
Know when to fold 'em
Know when to walk away
And know when to run
You never count your money
When you're sittin' at the table
There'll be time enough for countin'
When the dealin's done

When you think about that, it's great advice for playing cards *and* living life.

WILLIAM RANDOLPH HEARST

(1863–1951) American businessman and media mogul who developed the nation's largest newspaper chain and media company, Hearst Communications. He was the first to emphasize sensationalism and human-interest stories

Hello, Sandy.

Well, your latest book is just the sort of book I'd have loved. Allowing people to peer into the lives of others, the more famous the better. It's fascinating the nuggets of wisdom that can be gleaned by others in exposing the foibles of human nature. People are always curious and I, through my papers, lifted the lid on Pandora's box just a bit.

I suppose it's selfish of me to merely come to sing your praises and expect to be included. I should expose a few warts myself, shouldn't I? Frankly, I had so many imperfections I'd bore the lot of your readers, but what I can say with all sincerity is that I had no idea how serious our journeys through life really are, how much we must put up with in terms of human struggles and pain to learn very simple lessons on how to have kindness toward others and love for our fellow man.

Of course, here hindsight is perfect. Once submerged in a lifetime, all awareness fades and we're merely to play the cards with which were dealt. So, pointing out the real purpose of life should be of some value. To learn from those of us who thought we were pretty accomplished, but when judged against the real standard for living a successful life, fall short and are instantly humbled.

So, my friend, I'm here to show how ignorant I really was, even with my castle! We certainly judge others on the wrong set of standards, don't we?

Hope my insight enlightened a few. With a pure soul, I could have risen even higher, I'm certain of that!

With surprising humility and real admiration for your work, Sandy, opening all these doors for us and your readers. Good job! WRH

This next soul came after I thought every soul who wanted to be included was; I was wrong. You remember how these visitors tend to get my attention through electrical or energetic mischief. Four months ago, my car radio acted up. I have Sirius XM and for some reason the AM and FM bands were not accessible. I'd push them, and nothing would happen. I won't bore you with the routine service warranty versus the parts warranty details, but I took the car to the auto broker who set up my lease and then was referred back to the dealership. Of course, throughout that process I had to wait for appointments, but my schedule was so bizarre that I couldn't make the appointments right away. To confuse things further, the AM and FM came back on for a period of two or three days somewhere in the middle of that lengthy period, which caused a little rescheduling. Having spirits signaling me never entered my mind.

In late July, I drove the car to the dealership and tested the AM and FM bands to make sure they still weren't working prior to pulling into the service bay. The young service writer then jumped into my car and pushed the buttons, and guess what? They worked perfectly. I was stunned, and frankly, embarrassed. He probably figured I was some little old lady who couldn't quite figure out a silly radio in a car that was nearly three years old.

On the way home it hit me. It was visitors whom I had ignored for four months, still hanging in there. Later that day, I found there were three and Senator John Warner was one included in that group.

SENATOR JOHN WARNER

(1927–2021) American attorney and politician who was U.S. Secretary of the Navy from 1972–1975 and five-term U.S. Senator from Virginia from 1979–2009.

He may be best known for once being married to Elizabeth Taylor.

Dear Sandy,

Well, the lot of us truly messed up your car radio, didn't we? So sorry. Just so anxious to be part of your work.

I'll be direct and to the point. You might ask how could some senator from the South attract a woman as glamorous as Elizabeth Taylor? Likely men would like to know that secret, specifically, yet the same secret applies to all looking for a partner.

I was solid. I knew my values, had strong beliefs, and knew who I was. People seem to find security in that. I didn't jump around with my point of view in the Senate; I was consistent. I believe my colleagues respected that about me. I'd listen and evaluate but it was (my) core values that guided my direction.

I believe Elizabeth saw strength in an element of predictability, I had a beautiful ranch and she loved horses; plus, I was presentable in public. I'll have to confess, Elizabeth dazzled me! Still, it was being a solid, well-grounded person that allowed us to remain friends even after a divorce.

Thought I'd write something thoughtful about politics, didn't you? Well, thought I'd keep your readers happy. You have my respect, Sandy. Thank you for realizing we had been waiting in the wings!!

With warm affection, John Warner

JUNE CARTER CASH

(1929–2003) Five-time Grammy award-winning country singer, songwriter and wife of singer Johnny Cash.

Dear Sandy,

Well, what do you know? Isn't this grand? I'm coming to you with a personal connection stronger than some I had in real life.

That's funny. I don't even know you but feel like you're a sister of sorts.

I'm certainly nobody who is used to sharing their wisdom with others, not sure I even possess any, but I did live an interesting, if not challenging, life. If I could, I'd like to talk a little about helping others, loving through everything, and being loyal.

When true love exists between two people, the other one should be there to be a steady hand, if needed, and everyone needs help at some point in their lives. I wasn't one to judge. I'd be disappointed, I guess even angry once in a while, but it was always short-lived. Love always won out.

In my songs, I tried to convey how important loyalty is, sharing joys and sorrows with our friends and having fun, when it was appropriate. Music was the time I had the most fun. I loved being on stage and I felt the warmth and love coming from the audience. But mainly I felt the love they had for Johnny, and it just sort of spilled out over onto me.

I hope people who read this don't think I'm some silly old woman spouting on about being a wife and the importance of that. I guess, first, I don't want them to think that being a wife or husband is unimportant. It is the foundation of a healthy society—raising a family, celebrating, and worshiping together. It may sound old-fashioned today but there is nothing that makes a person feel more secure than having that sort of thing in their life.

So, I ask people to look around at the people they know who are the happiest and most content. I'll bet those people have a spouse and a marriage that has survived a lot. I'll bet they have kids, maybe not perfect kids, but kids they love and who love them. They have a family unit that comes together when it can, and they worship somehow. Perhaps at church or maybe just at home. But they know God and God knows them. I'll also bet they love music.

I think music is the thread that weaves the fabric of our society together. It shares history and lessons and stories. It is the one communication vehicle nobody is going to censor or cancel, or whatever you call that today. Music is forever and I'm proud it was the major part of my life.

Thanks for letting me speak. Johnny says "hello" and "good job" with your work. I think he'll always be close by me. ☺

Respectfully, June

F. SCOTT FITZGERALD

(1896–1940) Great American novelist best known for his novels depicting the flamboyance and excess of the Jazz Age, a term which he popularized.

Hello, pretty lady,

I know you know who I am and have read some of my books. You relate to that era; it was great and an exciting time: champagne flowed, sleek motor cars were all the rage, and everyone let loose! I guess it was a celebratory period!

I tried to be very dapper, a Dandy, I guess we'd have said then. You'd think me ridiculous today, but with Zelda, I had quite a spectacular life.

I never hurt anyone—maybe broke a few hearts by ignoring them, but Zelda was the one for me. I have few regrets, perhaps omissions and things I didn't manage to squeeze into my life. I could have helped the less fortunate more, but that's for another life. I made everyone happy with the wild parties we threw and through reading my books. I lived what I wrote and fantasized other parts. Not all bad, I guess.

I'm here because you do that, too. You write what you live. You and your son working as a team to help us all with your communication skills and his example.

Imagine, I can communicate once again with a "ghost writer" doing my bidding. ☺

Well, tell everyone to enjoy life. It doesn't have to be a drudge. Fun is everywhere and people are more personable with others when they dress up a bit, which is why we'd attend or throw lavish parties with lights strung, great live music, and everyone dressed to the nines. People have more confidence and behave at their best when dressed the part. So, every day, dress! Fix the hair and face, reach out and be prepared for laughs and adventure! It always comes.

Cheers, Sandy. Life is and can be for everyone a constant party if they surround themselves with the right friends! Scott

One sidebar to Fitzgerald's comments. Alcohol was his addiction, and he made no mention of his struggle with that nor how drugs and liquor may have played a role in the lifestyle he loved. Today, one needn't use either drugs or alcohol to do exactly what F. Scott Fitzgerald is advocating since even the Dalai Lama celebrates life routinely, evident by the joy he exudes and his continual broad smiles. We can *all* delight in this life, and friendships enrich it all.

ANNIE OAKLEY

(1860–1926) Phoebe Ann Mosley was an American sharpshooter who starred in "Buffalo Bill's Wild West" show.

Hi my new friend,

I didn't have many friends in my day; moved from town to town so traveling a bit with my shooting. The West was truly an exciting place and time to live. You'd have loved it. Unpredictable and adventurous. We never thought much about life. We reacted to what popped up in our path and how we felt in our body. When dead tired, we slept otherwise no need; we sat and rested and ate when it was around and whatever was around.

I suppose I was a curiosity. I was a great shot, and show-circuit life was fun and protected, really. Nobody messed with us because they all respected the entertainment value. Sort of a safe zone of existence. The only time we'd get shot was in a freak accident when somebody's pistol was pointed in the wrong direction.

I guess my lesson is find something to do that keeps you so busy you don't notice the irritating details of life that others get caught up in. It's the branches that poke us—the top of the forest is a soft cushion on which to float through life.

I know what I meant to say, and Sandy you captured it, so I am less rough around the edges. Never knew I was so articulate! Exactly what I meant, and I appreciate you capturing the intent in a way people will actually remember.

You're on target, my friend. Come join me up here and we can enjoy my Second Heaven of adventures and excitement of all sorts!
Annie Oakley

Nice compliment from Annie Oakley. I actually hear the full thought and see the picture of what they are referring to in the forest/trees metaphor. Guess I'm a blend of medium, intuitive, and smarty-pants— importantly, I know they trust me.

Ethel Merman was one of a kind. It was easy to remember her iconic performances on Broadway in *Gypsy* and *Hello Dolly.* I also can't forget her singing Irving Berlin's "There's No Business, Like Show Business." Ethel Merman wraps this section up by posing a challenging question to all of us.

ETHEL MERMAN

(1908–1984) American actress and singer known primarily for her distinctive, powerful voice and leading roles in musical theatre. She was referred to as the "Undisputed First Lady of the Musical Comedy Stage."

Well, Sandy, I guess I was bigger than life. The characters I brought to the stage were bigger than life, too. Big voice, big presence, and big life. It was all wonderful.

Not sure what my role really was there except to entertain, to bring joy where I could, and to help people pass the time with [the] *characters I portrayed who provided inspiration, example, and a dose of energy to some lives who were lacking that.*

Isn't it funny what the people in show business do? They become other people, they act out stories and they sing or dance their hearts out, really for acceptance and applause. I think there is something lacking with us. It is really more than a craft, it's a need. Boy, I must have had a big one.

I know you remember who I was, and I think you enjoyed some of my music and the roles I played. That brings me joy. Everyone wants to be appreciated and they can be in their normal lives too, if they are an example of something positive to their friends and families.

Maybe their gift is listening; maybe it's a natural humor; maybe it's some creative talent expressed in cooking, decorating, sewing, or gardening; maybe it's being kind and helpful or just loving the devil out of those close to them. Everyone, when they pass, will be remembered for something.

What do you think people will remember about you? A thought to ponder. Ethel Merman

Chapter 8

THE GAME OF POLITICS

Prior to the 2020 election, I watched more political news than ever and became totally depressed. So depressed, in fact, that I was questioning why I was living during this period when fiction was seeming to win out over fact and when accountability of politicians, important government employees, and elected officials was non-existent. The way the two major political parties attacked one another, unfairly; the obvious corruption of some individuals involved; the continual lying, not by the usual suspects but also by institutions we once trusted; and the bias of the media. Anyway, I was thoroughly disgusted and more so than normal.

Finally, after too much TV news, I turned it all off exasperated and switched to a movie. Then, exhausted, fell asleep. The next morning at 5:45, with a blazing light filling my bedroom, I woke up. It was coming from my TV screen: the VISIO logo shining through the doors of my armoire so brightly that it lit up the entire room. I shared this story earlier in this book and this was the occasion when not one, not two, not three, and not four, but five spirits decided to pay me a visit.

Finally, through the process of elimination, I determined it was three men and two women—all from Arizona and all in politics. Most I had known well, casually or had met in my life, but there was one I'd never encountered. An interesting mix: a city mayor; a state senator; a governor who was later a U.S. Senator; another governor; and a U.S. Senator who later ran for President of the United States. They brought with them exactly what I needed to hear; they all came with very uncomplicated messages dealing with political corruption.

Margaret Hance, the first, immediately apologized for the mess they created with my television. She was an amazing person but more importantly, extremely competent. Margaret was the first woman mayor of Phoenix, affectionately referred to by many as Maggie. She had a wonderful sense of humor and a reputation with a few who knew her well for loving a few cocktails. Anyway, like everyone else, I adored her.

MAYOR MARGARET HANCE

(1923–1990) First woman mayor of Phoenix, Arizona from 1976–1983; Republican.

Sandy, hi!

Remember me? Gee we made a mess in your life, didn't we? But we all saw you around political energy and your reaction to what is happening around you today politically. Your depression and sadness drew us to come help you through this.

First, nothing new! Do you think Mondale was a saint? Lots of corrupt cronies around him too, woven throughout the political world. The only difference today is the speed with which we find out [communicate] *today. Terrifying really. And then when shared with millions there is mass hysteria, uprisings, violence, depression, suicide!! Why do you think I drank? HA!*

[I was] *old enough to see it around me and helpless to do much more than a single person could. Maintaining my sense of humor was the balance for me.*

More to come from others! Sam's crowing in here. HA. Probably because you're still so pretty. ☺ Signing off, Maggie

STATE SENATOR SAM STEIGER

(1929–2012) State representative, state senator and mayor of Prescott, Arizona; Republican.

Hi Sandy –

Didn't know you well but Maggie is right, small cities or large, disappearing ballots, strategically placed polling places, gerrymandering districts—all part of the game. That's why politics is so ugly. People really get in to capitalize on the system and make money, have recognition, and act like they have power—80 percent, maybe. The balance are good souls who try. Some get burned at the stake, and others survive then run like hell back home when they retire!

Still, the fuel of the recognition is quite an aphrodisiac to many. Glad you never made it in. That would have been a waste of real talent, God protected you.

Too many of us for me to say much. Ernest is next. Sam

I knew Margaret pretty well but Sam only remotely since he dated a woman I knew many, many years back; occasionally we'd run into one another. Sam's reference about me "making it in" was a comment about my run for Phoenix City Council in 1989. I had a little time on my hands since the economy had taken a dive and my business wasn't keeping me busy enough, so I thought I'd add one or two terms on the city council to spice up my life. Besides, the man I was opposing had several issues so I thought the timing was right and I could make a contribution.

I likely would have won, if it weren't for a spoiler candidate from my same party who split my party's vote. Not surprisingly, it was the opposing party who talked this sweet, likable, and popular old guy into running for office. A smart move but even though the city council race in Phoenix was supposed to be nonpartisan, people knew who represented which parties. When two from the same party ran, it didn't take a rocket scientist to figure out neither would deliver the majority. Although I had raised more money than any other city council candidate to date, the incumbent retained his seat. I was probably lucky, at least Sam thought so.

One voice came after the other and now it was a man's turn whom I had never met, but I knew his daughter and son-in-law fairly well. Ernest McFarland had one of the most impressive political careers in Arizona history serving in all three branches of politics in the state.

I was shocked when Ernest referenced Sam Steiger's 80/20 rule: 80 percent were in politics for their own power and interests and 20 percent were in politics for the people they represented. Ernest McFarland's statement to that point made me laugh out loud since I had recently written a blog with these five people included titled: *Crooks and Crusaders: American Politics.* It was a perfect title and Ernest's opening line in the second paragraph, was the perfect reiteration. His openness and humility were charming, even endearing. I think I'd have really liked him!

U.S. Senator/Governor ERNEST McFARLAND

(1894–1984) Senator from Arizona, governor of Arizona, and chief justice of the Arizona Supreme Court; Democrat.

Hello, young lady!

Well, we never crossed paths, but Jewell (my daughter) is here with me and smiling so you must have been a good one. ☺

Well, I was one of the crooks. Not really, but my motives weren't pure. I capitalized on my knowledge and leverage throughout my political career. How do you think we got Channel 3 [KTVK]*? Leverage with the FCC. So, it's a game and if you think of it like playing monopoly, then it makes sense. Some rolls (of the dice) are lucky, some not, but when you land on a good square, you borrow money or do whatever trade you can to get a hotel on there!*

Over her [in Heaven] *it's not a huge payback in emotional pain since it's the intention that is what hurts the soul. Vicious, malicious, mean personal attacks causing pain; killing people for greed, power, or money, that's bad, bad, bad. A little graft or corruption when done with a playful attitude, not so much! So, everything is relevant: the century, the current society, the world dynamics, and the health of our own country.*

Shake it off. Watch less TV. Don't be ignorant but don't over-emotionalize or personalize. Just stay on YOUR path! It's a really good one.

Bye for now, more friends coming. Ernest McFarland

I was thrilled when I heard Barry Goldwater next. He was the originator of American Conservatism and had all the arrows in his back to prove it. Boy, people attacked him. He was outspoken, a bit brash, and frightfully honest. Frankly, I loved him. That kind of personality always appealed to me since I was a bit of a "truth teller" myself throughout life, and have a few holes in my back, too. At least we who live such lives are never bored.

U.S. Senator BARRY GOLDWATER

(1909–1998) Five-term Republican U.S. Senator from Arizona and the father of the conservative movement.

Well, well, well, aren't you the shining star? I vaguely remember you. You were involved and around, but boy, Sandy, do you have a cast of admirers over here! Jack Kemp, Harry Rosenzweig, Mal Straus, Burt Lewin, goodness. Margaret [Hance], *too.*

You don't have to do much to become noticed. This is the bit of wisdom I came to share, and it will apply to your wonderful and much needed book.

Original thought is a bitch! People clamor out of the woodwork to attack and question the source, the methodology, the feasibility, the intent around the effort. But you seem like a tough cookie to me, so you were absolutely the right one for this task.

I'll tell you, honey, I'll be here right beside you and I'll join your chorus of supporters. Hell, I'd have bought a carton of your books if I was there.

Keep your head down. Keep plugging through and don't let the political bullshit get you down.

Moving aside, but not away. Another voice behind me!! Barry

Governor ROSE MOFFORD

(1922–2016) First woman governor of Arizona, appointed, not elected; a Democrat.

Hi Sandy.

We did know each other, and I liked you. Smart cookie, which is why I put you on the Clifton Flood Task Force when I was governor. Brains. Everybody knew you were smart, but you were never cocky or arrogant. Just a problem solver, a doer, and always willing to help if anyone asked.

Politics for me was an accident, remember?

Rose became Governor of Arizona having moved up from Secretary of State when then – Governor Evan Mecham was impeached in 1988. I don't believe she ever had eyes for that job but played an acceptable role in the position into which she was thrust. I always liked Rose, but then, everyone did.

But I managed (key word here: not a leader, a manager) to make it through and serve the best I could. I was one of the 20 percent uncorrupt ones which is why I lived in an apartment much of my life.

Sandy, I was a caricature of a person: hair, eyelashes—but people liked me. You are not a caricature and people are often jealous of you, but once in a one-on-one [with you] *they feel your love and sincerity, then admiration takes over!*

You are doing amazing down there. Hidden a bit, but that's for now. Wait. More exposure. And you're right: get "who you are and what you believe" out there NOW so more will follow your blogs and your books.

Stay healthy. Big job, kiddo. I'm here, with love, too. Rose

After their messages, which rang so true to me—and amazingly, each made a different point—I slept that evening like a baby. All the tension had lifted, and I realized life is just life. It goes on year after year and even though societies evolve overall, human nature doesn't change all that much. A great lesson for us all, especially when we become disgusted with how the frailties of being human become magnified in politics.

Then, months later, another voice came with a spot-on metaphor that related to how politicians operate. It was Ed Koch, who was a fascinating guy and a lifelong Democrat. Ed described himself as a "liberal with sanity," and made that remark often during the 1980's through 2000's. Who knows how he'd describe himself today if he could see the way the Democratic Party has scrambled even farther to the left. His perspective is intriguing, as always.

U.S. Congressman/Mayor ED KOCH

(1924–2013) American politician, lawyer, and television personality best known as the mayor of New York City from 1978–1989. He was also a U.S. Congressman from New York from 1969–1977, a Democrat.

Hi Sandy.

Well, I finally got through. Lots of interference with me, likely because Satan has a lot of influence in New York's leadership (now). Of course, I'm going to talk about the state of my old state. Dreadful, isn't it? Who would have ever thought people would accept that kind of leadership?

Gee, I was affable but made sense in my leadership; sort of appealed to both sides. But look today: greed, despicable personal behavior, and I can't even say socialism in NYC; it's pure communism.

We here are all waiting for the world to wake up and shake off the shackles of control that have been applied to humanity worldwide. This is all nonsense and yet people more easily believe lies than they do the truth—someone wise said that. It was a good line, should have been mine (smile).

Politics is a combat sport and not for the faint of heart. One needs armor (wit and intelligence) for personal and professional protection; a sound body to lug all that around (values and morals) and to be nimble of foot to bob and weave through the landmines everywhere (flexibility and creativity). Then one has to be persuasive and an excellent communicator to boot. Not many fit that bill. Those not equipped to be true gladiators just ride in the chariot battles and let the popular spin of the day (climate change, socialism, racism, or whatever) carry them around. They ride in the popular transportation because they don't have individual legs to stand on.

Politics is a blood sport and it's time the public rise up to see a few drops spilled in accountability for grievous acts of some in the field. Without accountability, it's all for nothing. Without consistent rules of law, it is all for nothing.

Get smart, America. Don't look the other way. Use your voice, reclaim your power, and thumbs down to the bad guys!

Humbly offered (smile), Ed

Wasn't his gladiator metaphor glorious? You never know what to expect from these incredible icons. Their messages are all so extraordinary that I can't wait to see what they say in the next chapter!

Chapter 9

SECOND HEAVEN EXPERIENCES

By now, you're probably getting a rough idea of what the afterlife is all about; well, a general idea, anyway. There's the self-reflection portion that takes quite a bit of time drilling down from the obvious issues to the more subtle and finally the nuanced, while we feel the pain we caused others. Then, one of my favorites, besides the stereotypical Heaven, is the Second Heaven, as I call it.

In *"Hi Momma, It's Me"*, so many friends and family shared the encounters or observations that described their Second Heaven in magnificent detail. In this book, we don't have the bandwidth for exhaustive coverage of that subject, but these souls all mention that amazing part of the afterlife. I'll try to tell you a bit more about it, too, as the chapter progresses.

Ty Cobb's reference to his Second Heaven experience is so indirect you might miss it. It's how he begins the third paragraph of his message. Ty was not a deep thinker and was a man of very few words.

TY COBB

(1886–1961) American Major League Baseball outfielder nicknamed "The Georgia Peach." In the inaugural Baseball Hall of Fame ballot, Cobb received two hundred twenty-two out of a possible two hundred twenty-six votes.

Hello Sandy,

I guess I'm an old fogy to you (HA!) and you're probably an old fogy to the youngsters. That would make me ancient (to them)!

You probably imagine me in my baseball uniform. Well, our uniforms and bats were nothing compared to today's. The same with the gloves and the way they train!

I experience everything new [in baseball] *here as well as visit the first one or two ball fields more than a century ago. Heaven is the most amazing place—to renew, reflect, relive, and then to revel in the joys of this blissful environment. People never should fear death. It leads to this!*

They should also appreciate the gift of life and that's easier when you find someone or something with or in which you can share passion. Passion makes life alive. That is missing here, in terms of applying it [the passion] *and feeling the experience. Here we experience it as an observer only, not a* [physical] *participant.*

So, I'll move over now and let others speak. Not a lot to say but so happy to perhaps help someone with a word or two.

Thank you, my friend, for this opportunity. Ty Cobb

Ty Cobb's Second Heaven was not surprising. Seeing and reliving the experience of baseball from the very beginning and most elementary forms to what it is like today, and even perhaps in the future. Experiences on the other side are unlimited and anything is possible.

I guess we shouldn't be surprised by what Arthur Ashe is now experiencing either.

ARTHUR ASHE

(1943–1993) Only Black man ever to win the singles title at Wimbledon, the U.S. Open, and the Australian Open. He faced racism much of his life.

Dear Sandy,

I'm another African American voice for your work—not that anything needs to be race inclusive, but in the event anyone believes one single bit of writing in your next book is racist in any way, a few of us can confirm differently: Ray Charles, Red Foxx, Connie Hawkins, Jimi Hendrix, and myself; plus likely a few more to come.

I thought it a little odd that Arthur Ashe even brought up the subject of racism. But then, today, since everybody seems to use that term as a fallback term when they can't articulate a real criticism of something they don't like or understand, maybe he thought he should. I appreciate him qualifying the subject in advance. I appreciated his attempt to protect me; it was sweet.

Nothing I've come to say has a thing to do with skin color: only belief systems, which shouldn't be limited by any physical feature.

I reached the top and I was proud of my accomplishments. But I educated myself, trained diligently, and believed fervently that all things are possible with focus and a little sweat equity. A good lesson for all young people today.

I have no real regrets in my last life. What happened to me that caused my death was not of my own doing, but perhaps being forced to go public with how I contracted HIV, which developed into AIDS, perhaps educated others to be careful with blood transfusions. The industry woke up and took greater precautions and so I believe I contributed, even at the end.

I am thrilled to have an outlet with you, Sandy, and now we are connected in the event I feel compelled to share.

At this point, I asked Arthur if he could tell me anything about his Second Heaven experience. He was eager to do so:

Of course! What do you think? Tennis was my life, my passion, and my joy. I'm watching and playing with the greatest of all time—all genders, too. No sexes here!! All generations, in all physical conditions and on every court imaginable. Watching, playing, appreciating. It is joyful and it is Heaven - with much less energy expended - only the fun part!!

Again, Arthur's comment may seem like a conflict to what was said by one visitor before. Ashe mentions watching, playing, appreciating—although there is no physical experience involved—the emotion of what the players feel and even the physicalness of their actions is felt at an energetic level, a bit differently than here. Hard to explain but having read so many descriptors from so many others, the dramatic highs remain but the disappointments and any negatives are gone. One can't really appreciate the distinction over there since there is no bad to make us truly appreciate the good, but the essence of the core feeling and the bliss remains. I hope this makes sense.

I have no real lesson or advice to share except as I said earlier, all things are possible. I seemed unlikely to have the career I did, but I did. Anyone can excel at something to which they're called. Just pay attention to where you're drawn, what you're fascinated by, and what you look forward to. All really good signs!!

Thank you, Sandy. Enjoyed our visit. Signing off now, but will be nearby, Art[hur]

This is one more time when I tried to write the acceptable word, Arthur's name, and I couldn't write any more than Art. Nowhere in any literature is he ever referred to by that name, so I don't understand why he seemed to sign off that way with me. Regardless, that is the reason I spelled his name with brackets. I'm always true to what I'm given, even if it seems wrong.

Next is Dian Fossey, whose reference about her Second Heaven was brief, but I believe she was clearly referring to now being allowed to exist among every gorilla species that ever existed on this earth.

DIAN FOSSEY

...I have all my magnificent gorillas at every stage of their being from the very first to most current. Amazing! And I'm still in awe of them.

RAY CHARLES

(Postscript to an earlier message)

P.S. My Second Heaven is sounds. Not always music but sounds of all kinds that can be blended from the ancient to electronic to extraterrestrial. No limits here! It is Heaven.

As I mentioned earlier, those of you who have read my first book, *"Hi Momma, It's Me.": How Souls Stay Connected Forever and the Power of Undying Love,* there was a discussion on the Second Heaven experience in some depth. But for those who have yet to read that book, I'll try to summarize.

Everyone experiences the traditional Heaven that is almost too glorious to describe yet is exactly as you would image. In the Second Heaven, however, souls additionally have the freedom to "live" the passion they loved most in their past life. To some that might be being surrounded by nature; with others it is being with the animals they adored; with still others it is a particular sport like golf, race car driving, football or whatever, and to some it is art or sound. Those experiences could include any subject we could dream of.

That Second Heaven is only limited by one's imagination because the expansiveness of such encounters on the other side is almost unimaginable to us. One friend who loved gardening, greenery, and nature described his experience as being exposed to "nature on steroids" with leaves on the plants as thick as one's finger. Another who loved the magnificence of wild animals on safari is now able to observe not only every species conceivable but also the extinct.

Ray Charles mentioned sounds in a much broader context than only limited music. I can only imagine the sounds this treasure to humanity can now hear!

MARIE BOURGEOIS

(1870–1937) French chef who gained three Michelin stars from 1933–1937 for the modest restaurant she and her husband owned in Priay in the Ain region of France. She was only the second woman to obtain three Michelin stars.

Hello my friend,

This should be an interesting message for you since you are not much of a cook, only the simple things. I don't mean to insult you. but food is not your passion as it was mine.

It was actually taste and flavors, all flavors—the blending of them and how they disappear in some foods but enrich the flavor of individual ingredients. It is like a delicate dance of sorts. Some flavors linger on the pallet and others dance around the mouth. The texture of the food must blend with the art of the presentation and the extraordinary flavors. I adored food more than anything in the world.

I believe one must have passion and adore their craft to truly excel. Doing so, however, consumes one's life and I'm not sure that path is for everyone. We few are meant to inspire the average cook—like you, Sandy—to do more, to experiment, and to become more creative in the kitchen.

I have to say, I laughed out loud at Marie's comments about my talent in the kitchen, which is adequate, at best. I guess it's fine since I eat to live not live to eat.

You understand inspiration. You inspire others in your own way. There are other greats in sport who raise the bar, so to speak, to help others reach higher and higher. Only when we reach for the stars do we stand on the mountain top. That is what I did for cooking and for food.

Here, where I am, you cannot imagine the bliss I experience. My, as you call it—Sandy, my Second Heaven—is experiencing flavors and textures and aromas that are unimaginable. From all over the world, where I was never exposed during my life. Ancient recipes and blends, spices and methods to puree, to sauté and to mash which I never would have dreamed: using instruments which, in their own right provide a flavor. Divine, indeed.

I hope with this message, although not profound in any respect, I can challenge your readers to look around for inspiration in their life, study it, grab onto it, expose themselves to more of it, and let that help shape the life they will live in the future. The life experience is so rich with such encounters, and one must live life to the fullest. No?

Most humbly, your friend, Marie

It was truly funny when Marie insulted my cooking. HA! I do alright when it comes to large, family holiday dinners but, since I live alone, I spend as little time as possible in that one room of my house. It's amazing how forthright each of these souls are. They speak truth without hesitation. That's why I love hearing from them.

ESTHER WILLIAMS (2 of 2)

(1921–2013) American competitive swimmer and actress. Unable to compete in the Olympics because of WWII, she joined Billy Rose's Aquacade and did synchronized swimming and diving even in films.

I was never a profound thinker but can share my Heavenly experience. Guess what it is? Water! Swimming, watching magnificent fish, and bathing in and exploring all the glories of the bulk of Mother Earth's surface. Perhaps I was given the soul of a fish. But seriously, I did love playing, dancing, and even competing in water. Now I have it all, infused with unimaginable bliss.

You'll come join me when you come home, Sandy. I'd love to really meet you. EW

This chapter will conclude with a woman who was unique and courageous, especially for the time in which she lived. Annie Oakley, the sharpshooter who travelled from town to town with Buffalo Bill's Wild West show. There is no doubt her life was exciting and the times unpredictable. I can just imagine her Second Heaven experience.

Come join me up here and we can enjoy my Second Heaven of adventures and excitement of all sorts! Annie Oakley

Loved her invitation. And although her description was pretty simple, it does allow for the mind to wander, doesn't it?

Chapter 10

WARRIORS SPEAK

Throughout history there have always been great warriors, some famous and some infamous. I was honored to have several of them show up over the last few months. I'd categorize some as theoretical warriors and they are scattered throughout other chapters of this book; they include Golda Meir, Mahatma Gandhi, and Mother Teresa. The souls featured in this chapter, however, I'd describe as quintessential warriors for a cause, whether the cause was just or simply selfish.

This group presents a vivid contrast in personalities with each the antithesis of the other: from a brutal conqueror, a blustering but world-class statesman, and a military/political leader with an out-of-control ego, to a woman later recognized as a saint. Their diversity cannot be ignored, yet each of these one-of-a-kind personalities fought for that in which he or she believed. What unites the four here is the candid reflection and sometimes even regret they offer for the methods they used to gain victory and power over others.

ATTILA THE HUN

(circa 406–453) Attila, frequently called Attila the Hun, was ruler of the Huns from 343 until his death. He also led the Ostrogoths, Alans, and Bulgars, among others in Central and Eastern Europe.

Hello.

People feared me. I was strong and ruthless and had little concern for others. I made a name for myself but really wanted people to look up to me. They did since I kept them cowering on the dirt beneath me. That, I've learned, never builds respect but only fear. Fear is from the devil. Respect comes from those same subjects loving you. I was ignorant to all that.

I suppose I'm an odd person to come join you but people, all people, should know the danger of fear. Those who use fear for power or to rule, end up hated in the end. A terrible legacy—even family ends up being embarrassed for your deeds. Too big a price to pay, yet I see much of that in your world now.

If you put me in your book, maybe it will help someone open their eyes and begin to lead with strength and compassion. It's possible, I've since seen it in others.

You're a good woman, Sandy. I'm glad I came to you. I hope my words mean something and will be of benefit. Attila

JOAN OF ARC

(circa 1412–1431) "The Maid of Orléans" is considered a heroine of France for her role during the Lancastrian phase of the Hundred Years' War. She was later canonized as a saint by the Catholic Church.

My sister in spirit,

You, too, are a warrior, as I was. I saw the end and there was no stopping me to reach the place I needed to be. Men followed me, as they do you. I inspired them, as you do also. I knew the battle was my life and your life has been a constant battle, too.

I know more about you, as your life up here is transparent to us, and I still admire you. Often the less one sees, the easier it is to admire; not so with you. The more that's revealed, the more your magic is evident.

I learned about my life that a noble effort for the good of others is the best path for any life. No regrets. A sense of accomplishment and of course the ultimate act of execution for a cause let me experience the power of total submission, for good. I was always God's warrior. I believe you are too, Sandy, though we fight on different battlefields, [it's] *always for the betterment and salvation of others.*

I am at peace here. I did not return. I await your presence and you will be a good addition to our community of souls. Continue to spread love my spiritual warrior sister.

I'll fight beside you from here and cheer you on. So happy we have met. Joan d'Arc

As with most all messages I receive, I handwrote Joan's message. But by the time she got to the end I stuttered a bit with her signature. I intellectually wanted to write, after her first name "of Arc"—but that is not what I was forced to scribe. A lower case "d" came before Arc, which I didn't immediately understand until I looked her up online to retrieve her birth/death dates and a concise description I could use. Little did I know, she was born Jeanne d'Arc. So, Joan d'Arc was exactly how she would have signed her name.

This process always astounds me, as some signatures are more formal with a full name, others sign their nickname and still others, just their first. But, with each, the signature makes sense. Now Joan d'Arc's does too.

WINSTON CHURCHILL

(1874–1965) British statesman who was prime minister of the UK from 1940–1945 during WWII, and again from 1951–1955. He was one of the twentieth century's most significant figures leading Europe's liberal democracy against the spread of fascism.

Yes, I am here. Amazing how you see me in your mind's eye. In my suit with a big cigar, strutting around—on a beach, I think.

Anyway, it's never shuffling in a terry cloth bathrobe in worn slippers and needing a shave. HA! That was me, too. Human and very, very imperfect.

But I had one trait I'd never change and for which I was most proud. I had courage! Lots of courage. I was not fit enough physically to charge into battle as I matured, but my soul was as fit as an eighteen-year-old titan! Fearless, courageous, and tenacious. I hoped to inflict that image into the hearts of all Brits, so their strength of being would form a shield around our great country.

Leadership is about energy: conveying strong, positive, and relentless energy against the oppressor. Be that oppression from foreign invaders or a group of internal traitors. Organized evil is simply organized evil! We always fight against that.

As a soul up here, I learned my gruffness and quick temper hurt many and I've felt every bit of that pain, as we all do here. But if I had to relinquish any of my courage and fight in order to temper some of the penance I've done here—NEVER!

I appreciate how you've woven my words into your resilience keynote, after your son died. It worked well. And you have one leg up on me, Sandy. You were able to not only advocate for the immediate reward for tenacity, but for the extraordinary end result and catapult effect it causes if we have the strength to hang on and fight through till the end. I never recognized that while I lived. You do. A great lesson for all and very true.

Look at me, I could have backed down toward the end and been content with whatever reputation I'd built and tried to end more in dignity. But I was a model warrior, meant to lead and be an example, regardless of the personal pain during that process. I knew I had to follow through. The result? History has been more than kind to me and even you, my pretty one, used me throughout you're very meaningful resilience speech! Rewards abound!

Sometimes in life we can't help ourselves or correct slight—ha—imperfections in the course of our mission The eye on the prize, I say. Fight to the end. I did and wouldn't trade a thing in the overall.

Thank you for listening to my bluster and boasting. A bad habit, I guess.

BTW, your friend Larry Dossey [MD] *was right that our general personality comes with us over here; yet we all fit (together) perfectly. God's amazing work!*

Anxious to meet you here! It will be a joyous reunion when you can join us in spirit. Till then, we'll be your support team from afar. A pleasure making your acquaintance, my dear. You're one of the very good ones. Winston

Winston Churchill referred a couple times to the resilience keynote I was asked to present to a corporate entity in September 2018, only two months after my son's passing. When I told a couple of friends about this invitation, they both said *no surprise here!* My life has been a study in resilience, I guess, and when crafting the speech, I laced four different experiences together to make the point I wanted to make. The four experiences included a twenty-year struggle with an undercapitalized, fast-growing business I founded; two separate periods of time where I experienced groups of devastating illnesses—all of which I overcame without drugs or conventional medical therapy; and finally, the death of my one and only child, my son, Jon.

The consistent point in each journey was that if someone is truly resilient and keeps pushing through the event, however long that lasts and often past the breaking point, they will end up in a much better position than when they began the journey. In fact, a remarkably better position. The first, in business, where mastering my craft in developing amazingly successful marketing strategies for clients, I became so adept that I was able to package the process into a model for international corporations so they could withstand marketplace challenges. In health and healing, I became an expert in the holistic healing process; conducting workshops and seminars and writing the first holistic healing guidebook, ever. And, in terms of my son's passing, our new relationship spurred this mission for the rest of my life to build awareness among others of how souls remain connected forever and of the power of undying love. Books have followed.

That speech proved my theory over and over. It was impactful because, besides the underlying message and my personal examples, I enlisted the help of Winston Churchill by means of some of his amazing quotes. A couple of my favorites, although I used several, were: "Never, never, never give up.", "Success is not final. Failure is not fatal. It is the courage to continue that counts.," and "Success consists of going from failure to failure without loss of enthusiasm." And my personal favorite: "When you're going through hell, keep going."

It was wonderful sharing the stage with Winston Churchill; he was, indeed, the perfect partner and I'm glad he noticed the effort.

NAPOLÉON BONAPARTE

(1716–1821) French military and political leader who rose to prominence during the French Revolution. The Emperor of France from 1804–1814 and again in 1815.

Charge on! That could be the sort of message that is expected of me. Well, another surprise. I was known for being especially thin-skinned and retaliatory to compensate for my short stature. That was true: defensive, I'd say.

How silly of me. Here [in Heaven], *we can reflect and appreciate the beauty and uniqueness in us all. Some shorter in stature are much more handsome or charming or witty than taller, homely individuals. The sum of the components make up the man. Women also seem to be so inflicted!*

There are always multiple ways to reach a goal. Conquer through persuasion, leverage, and the unspoken truth that if battle were to occur, the other would surely be defeated. I believe you call that peace through strength. It can also be [by] *using that advantage to benefit many ways.*

Conflict in aggressive forms isn't necessary and, if we allow our own fragile egos to fuel such an effort, that burden lies with us and for that, we answer.

You surely have a collection of souls here: the noble, the brilliant, the lighthearted, the loving. And then there is our very much appreciated messenger. Thank you for devoting your time to us; we do still need to help others for our own healing. And, for the readers, who need to always pause and consider new information for their growth, too.

So, I'll end, Sandy, as I began. Charge on!! My dear friend, your army is here beside you to wage a loving war on ignorance and indifference. We applaud you—Napoléon B.

Chapter 11

THE SUBJECT OF RACE

Initially this chapter was created because I couldn't figure out what else to do with Red Foxx's comments. Older readers will recall what a controversial and irreverent comedian Red Foxx was, and Normal Lear's TV series titled *Sanford and Son* epitomized Foxx's personality. He said whatever came into his mind, was a little crude but very funny.

Foxx was true to form when he reached out to me. So, where to put his message was a dilemma. His opinions weren't those of a comedian reflecting on his life, instead they were the views of an activist fighting against the suppression of young Blacks.

Racism is such a sensitive subject today; it seems every time we turn around someone is calling someone else a racist. Too bad since the subject of racism is a serious topic and the throwaway references to it minimize its effect.

This chapter doesn't deal with racism per se but rather presents a fascinating look at the issue of race through the eyes of five Blacks who have more than a right to their opinions as well as two very surprising White men.

GENERAL STONEWALL JACKSON

(1824–1863) Confederate general during the American Civil War.

My dear woman,

Thank you for allowing me the privilege of visiting you and everyone. This is some honor and a real change of pace.

I suppose you're curious about the point in time in which I lived. It was dreadful. Man against man and in some cases family members fighting other relatives. Yes, some Northerners had kin in the South. The Civil War was bloody and tragic.

Fighting for a cause was noble in my eyes and Negro soldiers fought in battle too, for the North, to free the slaves in the South. Unlike today, where races seem to be against races, back then it was Whites against Whites fighting over the rights of Negros. I understand battles but I really don't understand war—no one wins in war. Losses on both sides! Eventually one surrenders, then the physical battles stop but hatchets are never really buried. The same injustice just takes other forms.

You'd think mankind would learn that political arguments, conflicts that result in wars, and battles never will end until we change our hearts.

You're right to preach love, Sandy. That's all there is here and it's just too bad we don't have memory of all this when we return to perfect ourselves (through reincarnation). It sure would be easier.

So, keep walking your talk and existing in the love you so ardently profess. That is the way—the only way to real peace.

With respect, [Confederate] *Gen. Stonewall Jackson*

FLORENCE GRIFFITH JOYNER

(1959–1998) Also known as Flo-Jo, was an American track and field athlete and the fastest woman of all-time setting world records, which still stand, in the one hundred and to hundred meters.

Hello.

I guess my message will be relatively short but directed to my Black sisters and brothers. In fact, those in any racial minority!

Forget the excuses. I was world famous and became so because I did something well that I didn't even know was a gift. I could run. Simple, huh? But every time I could use my gift, I did. I became more proficient each time until this little Black girl from a family of eleven [children]*... shattered the world record for running sprints!*

Endorsements followed, celebrity followed, doors opened to be [a] *spokesperson in commercials and whatever I might have wanted; to coach* [and] *to advise on product creation* [development]. *Didn't do them all but for a girl from an underprivileged background, that's a big deal. All because I could run.*

Pay attention to who you are, not what others may have done to you or those like you. Forget excuses. This life is yours to take or waste! That's my advice and I'd have listened to those who have been most successful, not the losers we may surround ourselves with.

No agenda for me. Just a soulful desire to help and offer what wisdom I learned in my life. God bless you all! Florence

RED FOXX

(1922–1991) A Black, outspoken American stand-up comedian and actor. His irreverent nightclub acts during the Fifties and Sixties eventually led to his best known, hit TV show, *Sanford and Son*.

HA! HA! HA!. Bringing you a little lightheartedness.

Sandy, I wanted to talk about what is going on in this country of ours. Our young Blacks are out of control, led, once again, by "The Man" and they don't even realize it; [they're] *just as stupid as they, or we all were as slaves. Born into it and just thinking that was our lot. Yet, it isn't! There are free slaves all around them and they see them as "house niggers"—still slaves, but in different circumstances. But they're wrong! These enlightened Blacks are free because their minds are free. That's the secret!*

When we can break away from the pack, listen and learn on our own, open up to consider what those "house niggers" might be saying, we can become free and enlightened, too. I'm not talking politics, that's a subject that's polarizing. I'm talking free vs not free.

First question, who's telling you to do what you're doing? Look around you: are they organizing you in groups, leading those groups to act, to believe only one thought? Whoever is leading you is the "Master." RUN.

If the others you run into in your life who try to tell you stuff as a young or old Black man, I'll bet lots of it is good, positive stuff about what's possible! New visions, exciting stuff. That's the path to your freedom!

Simplified: If anyone encourages you to band together to hate anyone or anything, run like hell. They want you enslaved and for you to do their dirty work. If the voices encourage your independent thought, throw out ideas or concepts—grab them, learn from them. They are giving you the keys to your jail. They're setting you free.

I'm a goofy old Black guy but I had a lot of wisdom, even more now. Don't waste who you are, my young friends. Run, run, run to your individuality, your potential, and your freedom.

Thank you, Sandy, for giving me a voice today! You are a blessing and in fact, you're like me: a freedom voice, for all! Love you, blondie. Red Foxx

I obviously didn't censor any of Red Foxx's comments; they were all his own. I know some terms might offend some but that is the way Red Foxx talked more than fifty years ago. Truth is truth and if you can wade through the off-putting vocabulary, you will see as I did, the truth that lies beneath. Red Foxx was a very smart man.

LENA HORNE

(1917–2010) African American dancer, actress, Grammy-winning singer, and civil rights activist with a career that spanned over seventy years. She was beautiful, articulate, and classy.

Hello Miss Sandy,

Throughout my life, I always felt like a songbird: a fragile, delicate bird who sang her heart out.

I loved my life and singing. It was what I was born to do. Perhaps I was given my looks to break color barriers. I had White features and darker skin. Men thought me beautiful even if they disliked most [others] *in my race.*

My music drew people closer to me and I always tried to behave like a lady: feminine, soft, and lovely. All women should strive for that regardless of their physical attributes. I believe people respect the effort to make the most of who you are: enhance beauty, develop quiet elegance, and offer some talent to the world. It's not that difficult. It begins with a healthy self-respect and a reasonable amount of pride.

So many women could learn that: Black, Brown, or White. Anger, brashness, ugliness drive people away and fuel discontent. Music softens hearts and beauty touches souls. Strive for that, my women sisters. Help unite the world again in love.

With a gentle spirit, Lena Horne

Lena Horne was the epitome of a lady who chose her words carefully, so people paid attention to her when she did speak. Her life was a lesson in class, and she lived a life that exemplified three old expressions: *less is more* as well as *you attract more flies with honey than with vinegar* and *speak softly but carry a big stick*. Afraid many of us have forgotten those sayings, but they may be worth remembering once again.

Although Lena Horne's career truly began in the early 1940's, throughout her professional career spanning seventy years, she seemed to have more access and to gain more acceptability than other Black performers. It was the delicate way she fused activism and politics with her art that made her unique. She was the first Black woman to sign a long-term contract with a Hollywood agency, yet she refused to play a maid in any of her films and she refused to bow down to the industry's skin color standards. Finally, the method Lena Horne used to fight segregation in the entertainment field and beyond was worth noting; she was an example of gentle pressure relentlessly applied, and in doing so, was very much an inspiration.

JESSE OWENS

(1913–1980) Olympic track and field legend best known for winning four gold medals at the 1936 Olympic games in Berlin during the Nazi reign. He mastered the high jump, long jump, and one-hundred-yard dash setting three world records.

This is a great opportunity to say so many things I've come to realize. I hope it will help other young Black men to realize their potential.

It's first: focus. See what you want or focus on what your talent is or you're good at and then just keep doing it. You will improve, you will get better; soon others will recognize your talent. That's the first step.

The second is consistency or tenacity: sticking it out. No one can improve or gain recognition or let that talent lead you to other doors which will open for you if you are a quitter. It's true, quitters never win. Seems simple enough but true. When it gets tough, that's when you keep pushing. Eventually you will break through the pain to a sort of ecstasy, an overwhelming feeling of satisfaction.

I didn't worry about the Nazis. I didn't worry about people being racists or not. I just did what I did. People discovered me and gave me opportunities for greatness in my life. We all can be great in our lives, in our own way, and at our own time.

Miss Sandy, you are another example of this. Thirty years you've been open? And now look! You have another world of admirers and friends. Life is a great blessing. We all have gifts. Don't waste them and quit letting other people in life, or causes, distract us. I hope my young Black friends hear this!

Thank you, my new White friend! Ha! Jesse

Now, here's the second White guy in this chapter with reflections you might not expect. In the event you don't remember George Wallace, he was the voice of segregation in the South as the fortieth-fifth Governor of Alabama at the height of the race riots. Alabama is the same state where Rosa Parks made her mark. I can still see George Wallace vowing "segregation forever" and blocking the door to keep Blacks from enrolling at the University of Alabama in 1963. I was stunned when he came to me while working on this chapter.

GEORGE WALLACE

(1919–1998) Five-term governor of Alabama and the third longest serving governor in U.S. history. He was a staunch segregationist who supported Jim Crow laws. He became a born-again Christian later in life and then modified his stand on segregation. He was a Democrat.

I'm here Miss Sandy.

Well, today any statue of me that's up should soon be coming down. That's if people remember some of us old Democrats and how racially insensitive we were. Yet, I believe these folks like to go further back so there is no political trail to tie to their (current) supporters.

It was tricky to live in the South and not consider Blacks to be much more than people to serve us. We were mainly raised that way, even those who went to church and should have known better. It was a disgusting part of our history but from what I can see it's merely a shadow of its former self. I don't see how the Democrats today can say we are more racist than ever. That's nonsense.

[Senator] *Robert Byrd and I were lightning rods for discourse around race-related issues, primarily bussing and segregation. Yet, both of us managed to make it through our lives pretty much unscathed. That was then, this is now.*

I'm afraid Democrats have a short memory for we (Democrats) were the ones who fought for slavery, not against it. We were the ones who wanted to keep Blacks from voting, not advocating for their right to do so. We were the ones who joined the KKK, not those who forced Klan members underground. Yet, Democrats today are the ones standing on their soapboxes being "holier than thou."

I've learned, you see, and even in later years, when I found Jesus Christ, I began to change. Now, there is only love for all: for Black, Asian, Brown, White and every hue in between. We are a culture of oneness and stupid people don't see that. We are united by blood that we give to each other through blood banks, organs we donate to save one another's lives, our own blood, which runs red like everyone else's and the common spark of creation that resides in us all. In Heaven we are only souls. There is no distinction whatsoever, which makes the entire subject of race irrelevant.

My advice to Democrats today is not to throw stones unless you want someone to look up the history of your own glass house. Democrats should lead on retributions, if there is ever such an allotment, and should be atoning for the sins of their fathers more than looking for little nuances in others to point at in vain.

Such a ridiculous fight, this race issue is. Please stop focusing on it and stop talking about it. If we do that, it will fade away just like prohibition did and other ridiculous beliefs that have and had no place in our society.

God is glorious and good. He is sad when he sees his children hating one another. I hate no one, I feel no better than anyone and I have paid dearly for the life I led. I see how wrong it was and how my beliefs hurt others. Forgive everyone, forgive yourselves and start over.

With sincere love for all fellow man—George Wallace

ROSA PARKS

(1913–2005) An American activist in the civil rights movement. During the Montgomery bus boycott, she refused to give up her seat on the bus for a White passenger. She was known as "the mother of the freedom movement" and "the first lady of civil rights."

Miss Sandy,

I'm Rosa Parks. I guess I became famous for just doing the things I believed in. There's power in following your beliefs.

I came to caution young people today that they have been led astray. We never overcome with violence. Violence locks us up in anger and fear and we become jailed for a long time; not literally but figuratively. Jailed in our minds and hearts, locked away from love and society and all the wonders life holds.

I'm so saddened by the anger in young Black hearts and young White hearts trying to relate to struggles that were never theirs. Anger is evil. Love and peaceful protest are the only ways forward, but we must be sure of what we're really fighting for.

For me it took a lifetime of racial strife. I knew why I wouldn't budge. Today it's a fifteen-second flash on the news, emails, and social media posts to get you worked up and the rallying cry that people follow with no substance for their belief; no real substance. Just edited stories, myths, and phrases repeated over and over.

That's not enough to stir anger, [but] *it should only be enough to stimulate curiosity.*

To some now, I'm just a silly old Black woman. But I'm more. This message is coming from all of us who knew how it used to be! It's so much better today with 90 percent of Americans treating us equally. 60 percent would be enough for the majority. That's enough. Be content. Forget gangs and mobs; make your own way. Find your own success and life.

We all paved the way and now are watching you. Make us proud. Rosa Parks

Chapter 12

JOURNALISM TODAY

For more than a decade I've been very critical of the way the media reports the news. Regardless of which side of politics you find yourself, it's impossible to ignore the bias of the media from either perspective. Bias is fine for columnists and commentators but not for people professing to report the news as journalists.

I've had a long life and of nearly four decades interacting directly or indirectly with professional journalists as someone who owned a full-service advertising and public relations firm. The media always had a slight liberal bias, but not like it is today. Today, talking points are predictively repetitive and the prejudice is disgusting. So, at this stage in my life, and with my background, I have a right to share an opinion on this mess.

The news industry has steadily declined in its attempts to put a lid on advocacy while attempting to report facts. They've also failed at accepting accountability, and tragically they rarely post retractions when they've been dead wrong on issues.

I've been so frustrated by all of it that a few months ago, I said out loud, *I'll bet Walter Cronkite is turning over in his grave.* In fact, I've said that more than once. Most recently, my patience had reached the boiling point when I decided not to watch any more TV news for a while because I was tired of hearing the opinions of commentators. Not long after, I had another "visitor"; it was Walter Cronkite.

Walter Cronkite was the most trusted man in TV news for decades. Ironically, he came twice to me about the state of journalism today. Later in this message, Walter refers to my early years when in grade school we all made a *ME BOOK*. We assembled multiple pages of different color construction paper, fastened with old-fashioned, silver round brads we'd punch through the paper, and then spread the two legs on the backside to hold the pages tight.

Anyway, on one page we were to draw a picture of our family, on another page any pets, on another page we were to illustrate what we wanted to be when we grew up and so on. On the "when we grow up" page, I drew a news reporter. This very professional looking female wore a tailored business suit and was holding a pad and pencil. I fashioned her after Lorelei Kilbourne, the reporter on the TV show *Big Town,* and even wrote Kilbourne's name at the bottom of the page so people would easily recognize her profession.

Funny, as the years passed, I ended up on the other side of journalism working *with* reporters not *as* a reporter. But I always was curious and loved digging into the who, what, where, why, when, and how of a story, subject, or product. It was product fascination that made me particularly good in the advertising/public relations field.

Walter must have seen that episode in my life within my energy field and his mention flooded my mind with very fond memories of an idealistic, small-town Midwestern girl, about eight or nine years old. That flash goal now seems slightly prophetic since now I am reporting, in a fashion, and taking every word down from amazing souls who chose me as their messenger.

WALTER CRONKITE (1 of 2)

(1916–2009) American broadcast journalist who was anchor of the *CBS Evening News* for nineteen years. A legend who was often cited during the 1960's and 1970's as "the most trusted man in America."

Good Morning, Sandy.

I guess you'd be curious about my take on the state of affairs in journalism today. It's so sad. No integrity, no individual pride in their craft. The professionalism has been lost. It truly breaks my heart because real newscasters, journalistic reporters, and even anchors of more soft news features or local news were dignified, respected, and in some cases revered. Now, they're like carnival barkers, one out-sensationalizing the other.

We had few, if any commenters in the old days except for Andy Rooney and he was great and Paul Harvey, too, who added color and depth to stories or dug down into the details to reveal facts, always facts, to prove a point or just make people think. Then the reporters in the field like Mike Wallace, in the early days, even Christiane Amanpour were in war zones reporting what they saw, not what they were thinking.

Although Walter didn't make a real distinction between Andy Rooney and Paul Harvey, they were quite different. Paul Harvey did report the news and then in his "Rest of the Story" segments, he'd drill down into the backstory of an issue or into what surrounded a person, which was always fascinating. Conversely, Andy Rooney, was definitely a commentator with very strong opinions which he voiced with great enthusiasm. America loved him because he seemed to reflect the values of most people in the center of America.

Remember, Sandy, as a little girl (third grade?) you wanted to be a reporter like Lorelei Kilbourne. Ha. Now look at you. Reporting the big stuff!!! This assignment, kiddo, is not for sissies. "Shoot the messenger"—remember—so write and duck!! ☺

I haven't any more to say, my friend, except to say I'm not spinning in my grave over this. It's worse than that. I can't watch anymore the career I loved and devoted my life to. Brett Baer is good—can't think of any others now.

Keep objective, Sandy, and report your heart out. My colleague and new friend, now, forever. Walter C.

Those reading Walter's second message might remember that he was the man everyone tuned into when John F. Kennedy was shot, when the first man walked on the moon, and every other story that was history-making or life-shattering. Cronkite was once the most credible voice in America. Many decades later, Arizona State University named their journalism school after Walter Cronkite.

WALTER CRONKITE (2 of 2)

Sandy,

I've come again today because I want people to know how I feel, what journalism was meant to be, and how it has all gone awry.

Today, we have journalism no longer. I guess that won't mean much to young folks who never knew who I was. But to those who remember John F. Kennedy's death or who have any involvement in the Cronkite School of Journalism at Arizona State University (ASU), they should. I represented, I guess, an era where newscasters were professional, unemotional, and reported what happened. They did not offer commentary on why it might have happened. They didn't embellish or dramatize and certainly didn't inflame as they do today. Most all the newscasters [now] *who profess to be journalists do.*

First, there should be an honest distinction between a commentator and a journalist. Yet today it seems alright for a professional journalist to color their coverage with opinion. That is not proper or acceptable in any form. Just as unseemly are the directives that come from news directors or station or network owners to slant the news for some political purpose. That's disgusting.

When real journalism existed, we all had loyalties and biases but were proud of how they never showed. No one seemed to know anyone on TV's leanings. Most of the leading newspapers strived for that, too, but that's where opinion pages came into play.

I am ashamed of our industry and if all this is now acceptable in journalism schools across the U.S., then I am truly heartbroken. It is my prayer that ASU has not let a corrupt group of radical advocates mold young minds with this destructive type of curriculum. Our free society depends on unbiased and a free press and media. There are venues for opinion, but the news desk should never be one of them.

Most sincerely, Walter Cronkite

Walter Cronkite and those of his kind reported the news with an objectivity that made you believe them. It was pure, devoid of ego, opinion, and emotion, and was delivered with an honesty about it that people could feel. That must be why he mentioned Bret Baer, who is ironically on FOX News, but his delivery is right down the middle with no emotion, and he is often picked to moderate political debates for that reason. I suppose the only way to regain any of that with journalists today is to remind them that giving their opinions is counterproductive to their craft. Actually, it might be helpful for journalists today to take a course in keeping their mind quiet, living in the moment, and simply passing along the information. That would be particularly helpful when they are interviewing guests and have a tendency to talk over them.

A woman journalist also showed up much later; her name was Marlene Sanders. Marlene was a professional, too, and was the first female network news anchor; so, you can believe she was serious about her craft. Marlene speaks to young people who might want to enter the field of journalism today. I don't mean originating YouTube videos out of their basements, but a real, credible position with a network, local station, or cable news channel. In the case of those positions, Marlene's advice applies and is a historical flashback on the way a career in journalism was supposed to be.

MARLENE SANDERS

(1931–2015) Trailblazing American journalist, and in 1964 became the first female network news anchor.

Dearest Sandy,

Well, you finally figured out who I was. Although quite a pioneer, I don't think anyone today even recognizes my name. I was everywhere in the TV news world, a field reporter, internationally and locally, a producer, and then I sat at the anchor's desk. In those days a person worked his way up, even Mike Wallace. Funny today how young people think it's different. All this quick, quick instantaneous fame that the Internet has brought to society has destroyed craftsmanship, mainly by destroying the concept of realistic expectations.

Frankly, this may disappoint a few of your readers, but no one graduates from journalism school and ends up on a news desk [TV], *even in a small market. Everyone works their way up. Sometimes if they are lucky, they get a few on-camera assignments out in the field, reporting on local events, traffic accidents, local fires, or whatever. Depending on how much the camera likes them (not glamour, but believability), they get a little more airtime in the field. Some help write stories and others help produce the newscast or soft news features. Only those with a strong camera presence—that X factor of credibility and believability—ever make it, even on a local newscast.*

But that's OK. If you adore journalism and the news business, there's nothing wrong with being a writer, an investigative journalist (part of a team), or a solo investigative star. Perhaps you have a face for radio ☺ *or have the wherewithal to do your own podcast. Still, there will never be instant success.*

Paying your dues is just part of making it to the top of any career you could name. Paying your dues sometimes looks like working around the edges of what you really want; sometimes it looks like practicing and practicing with the skill you were given; or sometimes it is instant excellence (perhaps in writing) but knocking on door after door after door until someone either publishes you or gives you a break.

I'm here to help manage the expectations of younger people today. Believe me, the fun is in working for it, not actually doing it. My most joyous years were digging out the story and putting the right spin on the production elements of a show (who to include, the points to be made, which visuals were most important). I always wrote my own stories, and later newscasts, but believe me, others had to approve everything! The glamour came later. But if you love what you are doing, the learning and growing in a field you enjoyed is the fun part.

Right now, Sandy, you are one heck of a producer on this effort. The good news is you don't have to talk anyone into participating—we all can't wait. It's like you found the sweet spot and we all showed up. What you are doing for us, allowing us to voice so much we may have forgotten, or didn't realize the importance of at the time. Now, we can speak about our lives and perhaps still do some good. That's glorious.

For those on the receiving end, you're providing a chance to be educated on the practical level, the emotional level, and absolutely the spiritual level. To get to know God in a different way through the magnificent humans that were Divinely created.

Thank you, my producer friend. You are a master! With professional respect, Marlene

Chapter 13

DEALING WITH CONTROVERSY

In the afterlife, being considered controversial is nothing for which we have to repent because controversy is so subjective. The definition of controversial can vary from one person to another, so being a polarizing figure, unpopular or what some might call "under question," or even "suspicious," doesn't quality for contrition on the other side. Being any of these might be undesirable, but it isn't a sin.

To clarify further, in today's culture some people are labeled controversial because of political leanings, personal style, or ideological differences. The perfect example is America's Forty-fifth President of the United States Donald J. Trump. Whether you love him or hate him, there is no question that he is still a lightning rod whose lack of political correctness makes him a dire enemy to the left. Opinions about him are always either black or white.

Others who qualify as controversial are a range of characters spawned from popular conspiracy theories, even though some of those theories have turned out to be legitimate, over time. Still, a percentage of the population is infuriated by the mere mention of their names, which is why one of them, John D. Rockefeller Sr., is also included in this chapter. Globalist banking families and early titans of industry often qualify for the list of powerful individuals who earned some disdain from the far right.

With that said, both enemies of the left and far right are included in this chapter, so I'd say my political bases are covered. This is important since in this book, I take no position on anything. I merely receive and communicate what is sent to me and I continue to be a clear vessel, communicating without judgment, exactly what I hear. Once in a while an annotation is made for clarity but not for reinforcement. Throughout this chapter some comments might be surprising and sometimes they make total sense when considering the source.

I guess I was a little surprised that more than one or two souls mentioned Donald Trump, but these messages were received at the end of his fourth year in office and prior to the Biden administration taking office. If you remember, throughout President Trump's first term, the news was filled with anti-Trump or pro-Trump commentary, twenty-four/seven. So, I suppose it was impossible to ignore such a commanding presence in our society or on the global scene from anyone from the other side who glanced over to see how we were doing. One simply couldn't miss the energy of Donald J. Trump.

I hope, regardless of your position regarding Donald Trump's presidency or John D. Rockefeller Sr.'s influence in today's globalist interests that you will read each of the messages thoroughly, remembering that these souls have nothing to gain by whatever they say now that they reside in the afterlife. You might find a few of these messages unexpected!

PRESIDENT JOHN F. KENNEDY

(1917–1963) The thirty-fifth president of the United States from 1961 until his assignation. Often referred to as JFK, Kennedy was charismatic, and he and his wife Jackie brought "Camelot" to the White House. He was a Democrat.

Dear Sandy,

I guess I'm coming through strong. Is that correct?

Well, we're supposed to connect so I can bring you some clarity on everything you've been hearing about my death, my intentions, and really who I was. I'm happy you supported me —so young and the glamour of Jackie and me, I get it. Still, I think your heart heard me when I spoke.

I was a true patriot. A man cannot serve in the military with honor without feeling a profound devotion to America. I felt it when I served and throughout my life. My father's motives may have been more power hungry but mine were not.

The stories about my intention to return to the gold standard were true. The global initiative, or the elite group around the world who wanted to control the world economic system, did not include my family. I had no loyalty to that. In fact, they shunned my father in private because he was an Irish Catholic. My position, however, was not for revenge but it was what was best for America. Why else would I have sought to put a man on the moon? U.S. superiority, that's why; and to express our greatness to the world.

That initiative [gold standard and global] *did me in but may have eventually put into force pieces that one day will overcome our economic collapse. If voters ever knew what methods and motives were in the political world, they'd be sick. Good thing they didn't. You needed a critical mass to defeat this. By the way, my family never got this, but Trump is my kind of guy. A Kennedy Democrat.*

I tried to be a good man, to be the son in my father's eyes [like] *Joe was, but it's hard to compete with an angel! I wasn't ruthless but I was revered, had beautiful women always around me, and had the wife my father thought was ideal—and she was. Much of my excess was a release valve to balance my constant back pain, my lack of energy (adrenals), and the stress of the job. Playing golf and lifting weights didn't suit me. Women did!!!*

Sandy, I hope I brought some clarity to all of the information you and others have been receiving. I'm sorry I couldn't stay longer to complete my work, but Trump is a good handoff for that. Boy, did that take a while! Hopefully he can still do more. He's smart and fearless.

Thank you for hearing me out. We all support you and your work. Quote me as you wish. We all trust you over here.

Take care of yourself, Jack

President Kennedy references a familiarity with material I have read about his assassination and about much of the global elite. I, like you, probably receive myriad of emails week after week, some related to political interests, some not. I try to quickly glance through all of them. Over the years, I've seen information that indicated the Warren Commission Report on Kennedy's death was created as a distraction to keep the American population ignorant to what might have been the real reason for our thirty-fifth president's assassination. We can't possibility believe all of government has always been and is transparent. With that said, in his message, President Kennedy shared what he wanted to about his life, his death, and his beliefs.

PRESIDENT HARRY S. TRUMAN

(1884–1972) The thirty-third president of the United States, serving from 1945 to 1953. Originally from Missouri, Truman implemented the Marshall Plan, Truman Doctrine, and NATO. He was a Democrat.

Hello young lady,

I know you like me, and I like you, too. You are outspoken and [a] *bit irreverent and so was I. There is something about Midwest values and being raised by the common man that gives one a perspective on life grounded in good common sense. I was proud of that.*

I was a courageous president, I guess. I knew the buck stopped with me so I couldn't afford any foolishness under my control. I spoke up and made my voice known and my intention clear. That is a mistake today with all the political-speak that goes on. People don't even know who they voted for once that person gets in office. Well, not sure they know who they are voting for before [that] *either, because few put their money where their mouth is. Few follow through and do what they promise.*

Donald Trump was sure the exception and I think he was the president most like me, that followed. He really didn't care what people thought, as long as they knew what was really going on. I guess there are too many filters on reality today: people wanting you to believe one thing or another, depending on who is in office.

I'm glad I'm dead, really. Too much silliness for my temperament. Hell, I probably couldn't even be elected to dog catcher. Not sure I'm supposed to say Hell, anymore over here; but God knows my heart and that I am merely an expressive individual. ☺

I hope a few old folks miss me. I'm just hanging around up here with Bess and those I love or liked a lot. Don't mess with too many others. Have my own work to do on myself.

Soul work is fascinating, Sandy, but I think you have a pretty good handle on all of that. You and your son (I like that one, too) are doing some meaningful work and I applaud your efforts.

I didn't have a lot more to say. I was never one to ramble on and on and on. I tried to pack as much as I could into a few words but speech writers or editors, especially when you're president, cram everything in there they think people should know. So, I went along with it. I really wasn't that hard to get along with.

So, my dear friend, I'm going to leave you now with just this one parting thought. When in doubt, call a friend in the Midwest and ask what they think! Bet they'll have a simple and very logical view of the whole thing.

Thanks for including me in your work, Harry S. Truman

MAHATMA GANDHI

(1869–1948) Indian lawyer, anti-colonial nationalist, and political ethicist who employed nonviolent resistance to lead the campaign for India to gain independence from British rule.

I bring greetings to you, Sandy, because you are trying to bring peace to others in your own way. Peace inwardly with oneself and peace, one-on-one with one's fellow man. Noble, for sure.

You are an interesting study in that you don't have one set formula or philosophy you follow, other than to love. But you adapt lessons each must learn to them... so they can apply the teachings of love and to rise above pettiness and fear to build a healthier more peaceful life.

I talked to the masses and got attention with my fasting or my hunger strikes. You, on the other hand, attract attention due to your striking appearance at a mature age. You are surprising yet articulate, and actually quite brilliant besides these new intuitive gifts. Oh, how I would have loved to have met you. Yet here we are.

I understand your father's family used to refer to your grandpa as me when he got his hair cut too short. He was smaller of stature and somewhat wiry, so perhaps there was a resemblance. I can't say who was better looking. ☺

I must insert this personal story which explains Mahatma Gandhi's reference to my Grandpa Brandy. Being raised by my adopted parents in Illinois, as a little girl I'd visit Grandma and Grandpa Brandy's home quite often. Grandpa Brandy was an immigrant from Austria years earlier, was a slight man, and was cute with his white crew cut. He was much older than Grandma and seventy-seven years older than me.

Anyway, Grandpa would walk downtown for his haircut and once in a while the barber would cut his hair way too short. When Grandpa would arrive home the family would tease him saying he looked like Mahatma Gandhi. Grandpa was oblivious to the whole thing, but I always giggled. If you don't remember what Gandhi looked like, he was of slight build, too, a spry little guy who was bald. They both wore rimless, wire glasses; Grandpa wore his less frequently. There truly was a resemblance.

I have heard you refer to me over the years, not directly, but when I tune you in over here that connection shows in your energy field. Small "infinity," right?

I didn't come to give advice or lecture anyone, more for acknowledgement. However, the world is sad and where I fought governments for India's benefit, all of you must fight the devil and evil for the benefit of your country, and therefore the world.

Today is the crossroads. Today humanity has a choice. Free will magnified, indeed. All of us here cheer on President Trump, a great leader of men and a voice for the forgotten. And we cheer on the USA.

I'm sending my blessings to you, Sandy. Your work is instrumental since you are laying the groundwork to shift others in your field more in your direction or focus. You have my support and yes, admiration. Mahatma Gandhi

PRESIDENT THEODORE "TEDDY" ROOSEVELT

(1858–1919) American statesman, conservationist, naturalist, historian, and writer who served as the twenty-sixth president of the United States from 1901 to 1909. He was a Republican until 1912, then ran again as an Independent but lost.

Hello Miss Sandy,

I suppose you've heard of me. Of course, in history. I hope all these years later your contemporaries respect my work and haven't gotten around to tearing my statue down.

Of course not, but it is quite a state of affairs in the United States, isn't it? That's what happens when a society gets lulled to sleep and doesn't recognize what's happening. The rise of Hitler comes to mind. Instead of one man, this time, it is raw power and greed, the most potent of aphrodisiacs that have brought together a collective of Marxist forces to take over. They don't necessarily want to overthrow one man; they just want to destroy whoever gets in the way.

And since this appears to be a global collective, the United States and your worthy president, Donald J. Trump, are the biggest targets.

I like Trump. We'd have really gotten along. A patriot, a fighter, and a gentleman, regardless of how the media has painted him. Rough talk worked for me because we were coming out of the cowboy era and Teddy Roosevelt and the Rough Riders stuck! Poor Trump is sitting square in the middle of your new politically correct culture so he couldn't sneeze without pointing that effort in the wrong direction.

[You have to] *stand strong. Stand loyal to your flag, your country, and your president. He deserves it. Whatever his choice here, stand by him. He was given a monumental task and will be looked on one day, if the re-writers of history don't screw it up, as one of the greatest presidents ever— in with a handful. How proud you must be to have witnessed his first term in office. That was legendary.*

Meanwhile, Sandy, I want you to know I'd give you a Medal of Freedom for bringing what you do to anyone who'll listen, the ultimate freedom to go past the constraints of religion, directly to God and to embrace <u>all</u> God's creations with the willingness to serve them like many have not ever been served, at the soul level, respecting their voice, and giving them a path to heal. I marvel at your work and the insight that brought you here. Freedom, indeed. A secretary to souls—a spiritual secretary, as you call it. But most of all a Divinely inspired messenger to help heal the world.

I'm proud to be among your throng of admirers up here. Pity those with no purpose in life. You have one in <u>spades!!</u>

Charge ahead my friend. You, President Trump, and me, all fearless and led by Faith and an iron will!!! Your friend always, Teddy

ÉDITH PIAF

(1915–1963) French singer and songwriter, cabaret performer, and film actress noted as France's national chanteuse. Her most widely known song may be "La Vie En Rose". She was revered in France and known as "The Little Sparrow."

I know you adore my work. Whenever you hear my voice, you seem to perk up. We must, and do now, have a connection. We are kindred spirits as you friend Rico says.

Her reference to Rico was regrading my dentist, Enrico DiVito, a very talented man who when I first visited him, I was in the process of recovering from my second bout of leukemia. He had just conquered lymphoma, himself, using different methods, but we were both fighters and had even more than that in common. It was the blood disorder history that led him to comment that we must be kindred spirits. I guess we were, since we've have remained friends ever since.

My voice was clear and pure. It was a loving gift from God and like Circe, I called people to me but in [a] *good and blessed way. A common soul with a great gift. We can't deny that God works through and selects unusual souls to do his bidding. My voice was always pure and communicated the pain, love, and joy experienced in this life. People could relate because I was not above them; I was not elevated. I was one of them.*

This was the gift, and just as President Trump has been chosen, you have been chosen. This is a crisis time on the earth in desperate need of communicating. Trump teaching, or rather encouraging, people to come together for love of country, and you, dear Sandy, encouraging people to come together in search of love they wrongfully believe is lost across dimensions.

Both of you use your voices as I did to do that. All blessed by the Almighty and never in fear but always in love.

I'm so happy to be in your extended family now, Sandy. When you hear my voice again, I'll be near, and I'll see your smile. Édith Piaf

PAT TILLMAN

(1976–2004) An American professional football player in the NFL who left his sports career to enlist in the United States Army in May 2002. He served in Iraq and Afghanistan, during which time he was killed by friendly fire.

Hi Sandy.

You can see my face, I know. Same photo plastered everywhere when I left. Guess it was memorable.

I want to address patriotism—how we need to reawaken that in each of us and how important that is! President Trump managed to light that fire in so many millions of hearts. I don't remember ever seeing so many spontaneous parades, flags waving, and people flying flags on or above their homes. Nothing like those four years, except homecomings after war and that took tragic loss to ignite such passion. Trump did it by his own enthusiasm, his action, and his love of the American people.

I'm proud of who I was, how I chose a life of service to my country over a life of celebrity through sports. I'm even proud that I could give my life in service, even though the situation was strange. It was still meant to be, and I was to become some sort of example.

I'm grateful to my loving family for keeping my memory alive. I still love them, eternally.

Thanks Sandy—you are the best and if I was there, I'd hug you in gratitude!! A great big hug! Pat

One More Controversial Soul

Another man, who appears to be facing disapproval from some is John D. Rockefeller Sr. I became aware of this animosity by some when I read the names of a few of the souls appearing within *Souls of Legends Speak,* I received a little push-back about including Rockefeller Sr. It appears some people think Rockefeller and his entire family were and are evil.

The source of that hatred stems from the Rothschild, Rockefellers, and Bilderberg group of families, who some say formed or were part of secret societies continuing to influence all the chaos and evil in the world today. More specifically, over generations their domination of central banks, slavery, legal and illegal drugs, politics, gang terror, violent overthrows of regimes, depopulation and the media have been poised to grab enormous power and to remake society through a new world order. The energy around their efforts for world domination, if true, seem to be the fallout because of their relentless greed.

This is my position on John D. Rockefeller Sr. and his right to be heard in this book. I don't judge. As with all souls who have come to me, I heard purity of intention, underlying sincerity and often love coming through in Rockefeller's remarks. You may find that as well. Once souls reach the other side everything changes and amazingly, even the most powerful become very humble. That's why he as well as all the others are I included. As you remember, even Attila the Hun was given his platform to speak.

I'll say a bit more on this participant. His first message is rather benign as he talks about being a visionary. His second covers his what drives many wildly successful men, which I thought, in context, was very honest and perhaps revealing.

JOHN D. ROCKEFELLER SR. (1 of 2)

(1839–1937) American business magnate and philanthropist. In 1913 he became America's first billionaire and is the wealthiest American of all time when amounts adjusted to today's dollar.

Hello Sandy,

My goodness, you're a busy one. Well, I'm the old, original Rockefeller. Somewhat of a visionary, which is why I'm writing to you. You are a visionary, too, aren't you? Most people have no idea what makes that work. So, I'm here to explain.

To be a visionary is quite easy. Simply let a vision come into view, but the rest is where it becomes tricky. To believe it's possible, to see how it fits and why it fits is the analytical piece; and to tackle the challenge is the fearless, warrior part. Some people have one or two elements but rarely all. You are unique, Sandy, as was I, for we both also see the detail it will take to bring it all into reality. Even with the first elements, without knowing who else to enlist, what other things it will take for success, and then having the tenacity to see it through is rare.

One component that is immeasurable but the most difficult, I believe, is being surrounded with one, two, or three people who believe in you! The vision is nice, but the entrepreneurship is key. I had a wife who did and a couple friends who came alongside. I guess I ended up with quite a family legacy.

In hindsight, I don't have any real regrets except I never knew how to receive like I should have. I was so busy pushing my way onward. Receiving is a tough lesson for many but look how lucky you are, my girl. You had the ups and later when the downs came, you learned. I think illness and vulnerability helped with that. If I could offer advice:

Know who you are.

Embrace that.

Believe in yourself and your mission with everything you have. It's contagious.

Sincerely, John D. Rockefeller Sr.

JOHN D. ROCKEFELLER SR. (2 of 2)

My dear Sandy,

I'm coming to you to explain the ego's impact on those in business and I'm talking about the entrepreneurs like Bill Gates as well as the international banker types and Wall Street types. Big egos are big egos.

The issue with them, and I was a bit like this myself, is they can't get enough. If they conquered an industry, they expand into others. If they are in the top handful in their industry or country, they expand globally for financial influence. Then it's rising to the top of that group. Competitive to a fault. And they use their partnerships and alliances only to expand their own personal reach of power. Truly isn't the money at that point since they couldn't spend all they have. Rather, it's sheer power. And they'd take less money to have more authority over decision-making and more individual prestige.

All this global stuff is run by massive egos. Davos [location of the World Economic Forum each year] *is the game board on which they play—like a giant Monopoly or chess game. Even their countries mean little. They'd sell out their countries' interests in a minute.*

Donald Trump took a whack at a hornet's nest on this one. Everybody has something on someone else and Trump may have opened Pandora's box. Not sure he can play through to the end on this one. He has done so much and shining a light on things could have initially been enough, but like all the others, his ego wouldn't let him stop. He had to reveal more, clean up more, and prosecute the criminals. A tough if not impossible job.

We all love his heart and know he has tried to save the U.S. In the end, there may be too many hornets and when it comes to surviving those stings, most people run! Continue to pray for Trump. He surely needs it now. We all love him. John D. Rockefeller Sr.

Once I read Rockefeller's second message, recalling the comments of a couple friends, I began to wonder if he was truly the mastermind behind much of the very questionable work of the Rockefeller Foundation as well as the UN, International Monetary Fund, the Federal Reserve, and so much more. I asked if he would come back to answer a few questions. Since he had shown up in my life twice, I thought it might be alright to ask.

He came without delay, and I posed the one question I had. I asked what his intention was for his family's work and the efforts of the Rockefeller Foundation after his death; he died at 98. This was his response.

> *The original intent (of mine) was world banking. Then, as more (people and family) got involved, the tentacles spread. Each had focuses that enhanced the power of the majority participating. All today's details were never spelled out when I was alive. I can't apologize for the sins of others, only explain the internal working of living man that might fuel that. That's what I tried to do with the second message I sent you. I hope that is helpful, Sandy.*

Chapter 14

PROFESSIONAL ADVICE

Once souls are in the other dimension they no longer worry about details like the bottom line, market trends, competitive issues, or how long a bureaucracy takes to approve a new drug or issue a building permit. These things are irrelevant when it comes to purifying our souls. The individuals contributing to this book now see only the forest and not the trees. So, it stands to reason this chapter has nothing to do with the specifics surrounding job performance, but rather has everything to do with the attitudes and philosophies that influence life and work. Attitude is always what fuels human behavior, and therefore, influences job performance.

Since most of us are destined to work in our lives, any suggestion would be helpful, right? Well, advice is even better when it comes from individuals who've mastered their field of endeavor and are undeniable winners. Some of their guidance will be consistent with their own career history, while other guidance will be more general in nature. Either way, hopefully you'll find pearls of wisdom that relate to a similar situation you're facing right now. It might even help you perceive a challenge you're currently facing differently.

Bud Abbott begins with his thoughts about partnering and teamwork; both which require putting aside one's ego for the greater good. Whether you're a C-suite executive, forming a strategic alliance with another company, a middle-manager in a large corporation, or one of a team of employees in a small firm, partnership and teamwork are part of the game.

BUD ABBOTT

(1897–1974) American comedian, actor, and straight man half of the comedy duo Abbott and Costello. Groucho Marx declared Abbott: "The greatest straight man ever."

Hi young lady.

Well, you seem young to me! I came to share a bit about my lessons and the values I now hold dear: partnership: sharing the credit, regardless of whose name comes first!

I guess you could say I was the brains, but Lou was clearly the talent! Unlike Martin and Lewis where Jerry was everything! HA! Anyway, in show business in the very early days, if you didn't have a great deal of talent, but had drive and ambition, you formed an act. Could be a guy with some dogs and a pretty girl, a singing group, or a dance group (usually two of three); and in those days there were many like that.

Today it seems everyone is selfish and looking for their fifteen minutes of individual fame, at anyone's expense—even their own. That's foolishness and always short-lived. Like great athletes or musicians, only the cream ever rises to the top, but with all the ways for people to garner exposure, flash in the pans appear to be everywhere. Even to criminals who commit horrific crimes to become a name people remember.

Lou and I worked hard, were humble, and maybe the young people today don't remember or know of us, but we did influence many young comics who learned from us the physical comedy and playing off one another. Look at George Burns and Gracie Allen (man/woman), Martin and Lewis (singer/physical comedy genius), the Marx Brothers, and of course us, too. We all made contributions and weren't afraid to share the spotlight.

I'd rather have shared the glory than never been in the spotlight at all. Generosity of spirit; willingness to partner and respect and kindness—it all goes hand in hand if you want a lasting career in any field.

Hope this helps or inspires someone, Sandy. Keep up the good work. You're really something! Lou

Learning to partner doesn't seem like a mind-blowing concept, but to paraphrase Lee Iacocca from the first chapter of this book, there are only so many lessons in life and we simply rehash and repackage those lessons over and over for a richer life. Napoleon Hill will say something quite similar in a later chapter. So, don't overlook the simple suggestions. They are quite often the most powerful lessons in life.

On that same note, if you remember, there was a very successful book from the 1980's titled, *All I Really Need to Know I Learned in Kindergarten: Uncommon Thoughts on Common Things.* Well, here is another simple message but they're always packaged in a way so that we can't totally ignore them.

JULIA CHILD

(1912–2004) American cooking teacher, author, and television personality recognized for bringing French cuisine to the American public with *Mastering the Art of French Cooking.*

Hello, my dear.

Wonderful meeting you, especially this way! A treat, indeed.

I had a fabulous life, adored my husband and of course food! I learned to cook so I could experience every imaginable flavor, and I wanted to share that joy with the world. I think I made cooking fun and the finest cooking a little easier.

It would have been a blessing to have children but not my lot in this lifetime. So, my babies were carrots, broccoli, cucumbers, and every vegetable I touched. I did treat them all well and in return they nurtured, me! How about that?

Sandy, your work is fascinating, and I know you'll encounter critics and rejection as I did. But I say to that, if one hasn't experienced rejection in life, they aren't aiming high enough.

We all believe in your work here, just as my wonderful husband believed in me. Let that propel you forward.

Onward and upward!!! Julia

Sometimes the wisdom these individuals share will come in the form of a single thought or sentence like Barry Goldwater's "Original thought is a bitch!" and Julia Child's "If one hasn't experienced rejection in life, they aren't aiming high enough," both of which are profound. John David Rockefeller Sr's "Belief in oneself is contagious" (slightly paraphrased) is another. All are so memorable and just a few of the very many this book offers.

HENRY WADSWORTH LONGFELLOW

(1807–1882) American poet and educator who wrote *Paul Revere's Ride, The Son of Hiawatha*, and *Evangeline*, among others.

Hello young lady,

I'll bet that's refreshing to your ears! We may be the last group showing up to be included in this great and fascinating book! My, you have courage to tackle such a task, but then again, you didn't have much of a choice, did you?

Longfellow's reference to being in the last group to show up for this book is likely true, as of this part in the final writing and editing since late July 2021, another impactful energy event occurred in my life. My range and oven began to overheat which caused a code to show on the dashboard. The oven would no longer work, and the top burners stayed hot without fluctuating as they normally would. Therefore, I couldn't use the appliance until a repair man came to correct the situation, which he did by merely flipping the breaker switch.

By then I'd figured out there were still more souls signaling me. I was right. It was five of them all at once and Henry Wadsworth Longfellow was among them. They assured me that they were likely the last, which was good since at this point, we had surpassed one hundred twenty participants. Just for your reference, the other four were Annie Oakley, Thomas Edison, Bonnie Parker (of Bonnie and Clyde), and Laozi also known as Lao Tzu. Those folks are scattered throughout other chapters. Now, back to Longfellow.

> *In grade school you leaned all the classic authors, but you seem to remember me best from the card game "Authors." Yes, I can see you picturing me with snow-white hair and a fairly gentle countenance. That portrait did capture my personality. I was not a man of extremes. I was a more professional and disciplined writer.*
>
> *Believe it or not, my message is quite short! One need not be mad, eccentric, or addicted to drugs or alcohol to be a profound and meaningful writer of prose or poetry. I was quite normal comparatively and lived a respectable length of time.*
>
> *So, you budding writers out there, don't think you need artificial fortitude to begin. Just begin. Be open to inspiration as to where or how to start, the general over theme, and then begin your process which will differ for everyone.*
>
> *Look how you've blossomed, Sandy. You were never driven to write. You were driven to teach through words. So there! One never knows, and if kids today scan the deck of "Authors" (is it even still around?), they'll find all sorts* [of us].
>
> *Lovingly, the white-haired one!! HWL*

I can still remember the beginning lines of "The Song of Hiawatha" by Longfellow: "By the shore of Gitche Gumee, By the shining Big-Sea-Water." Goodness that must go back more than sixty-five years for me, but magnificent writing remains magnificent writing. I did learn about him, among other great writers, in grade school.

The most prominent memory I have of Henry Wadsworth Longfellow is, just as he stated, from the vintage card game "Authors." Sadly, to answer Wadsworth's question, the Whitman version, which was the best, is now extinct. I don't think the game exists at all except a few partial decks here and there on eBay. Sad because I adored that game and it would be fun to fan out that deck, once again. At the time, the faces of those authors were branded into my young, developing brain, and, he was right, he was the white-haired one.

ROY ORBISON

(1936–1988) American singer, songwriter, and musician known for his impassioned singing style, complex song structures, and dark, emotional ballads—as well as black clothes and dark sunglasses to combat his shyness. You may remember "Pretty Woman" and "Only the Lonely."

Hello, Miss Sandy.

I guess some address you as that; it just felt comfortable for me. I haven't much to say other than music, real, individual music with its own identifying characteristic, will always be recognized and remembered.

My voice was unique and so was my style. I didn't attract all the ladies like some did, I wasn't sexy in that way, but people loved my music, and I was truly proud of my career.

I guess I want to encourage folks to not talk themselves out of success. "I'm not good looking enough, not smart enough, don't have the contacts or connections," and so on. We are our own worst enemies.

Just do what you feel compelled to do. Even if it's part-time or a hobby. If you like it, do it and keep doing it. Someone will see you, hear you, admire your work, and one thing will lead to another.

We block our own success with negativity. I never let people discourage me. I just kept trying. I did OK.

Well, that's about it from me. Your life will roll out as it's meant to, just don't make it hard on yourself. And, if along the way, you enjoy life in some ways, that's success.

Hope this helps someone. I'm not a deep thinker. Just a guy who was tenacious and loved what he did. With my best wishes, Roy

F. LEE BAILEY

(1933–2021) American criminal defense attorney. High profile cases included Sam Sheppard, Albert DeSalvo ("Boston Strangler" suspect), Patty Hearst, and Ernest Medina (Mỹ Lai Massacre). Later, he was a member of the "Dream Team" for O. J. Simpson.

My dear woman,

Kunstler kept popping into your head, didn't he? He must either envy my position (here) or be debating whether he'll pipe up. HA! I was better looking. ☺ (Humor is not dead here, my dear.)

It was true, before I was given F. Lee Bailey's name, I kept seeing whiteish hair and Kunstler's last name popping into my mind. William Kunstler was an American radical lawyer and civil rights activist who was almost as unpopular as his clients. He was also an unattractive man and lived well before F. Lee Bailey. Kunstler must have been hanging around but when I asked if he was my visitor, I was told NO. So, eventually the right lawyer got dialed in, so to speak. By the way, F. Lee Bailey was a much more handsome.

What a challenging life I had. It takes quite a bit of courage to take on the challenging defense cases I did because they were so high profile! I'd never have won any of them without a splendid team around me. I recognized that although none of my support team were ready for public recognition, the trial attorney is always the face of the defense, and a strong reputation gives one an edge with any jury. I was a winner.

My time was winding down by the time of O.J.'s trial, but with Patty Hearst and many others that followed, I was at my best.

I'd say if you have a healthy ego, and many careers demand it, it helps because one would never have total confidence without it. But confidence that's born from believing it's 100 percent your own doing is not good. In your heart, although you know you'll prevail with whatever it is, that knowing comes from being aware that God will give you the right setting, the right attitude, and the right words for the task. In your heart, it isn't raw talent, it's God working through you. To the world, however, you're invincible.

The ironic part of this is the more you believe in the invincibility of you (and God), it's always there.

His last sentence was awkward, but I believe he meant to say the more you believe in the invincibility you have through God's help, the more likely you set the stage for that being so. The way he phrased it was weird, but I knew what he meant. I just didn't feel right changing the sentence completely.

I was cocky, brash perhaps, and preened toward the camera, but always in a controlled, professional, and classy way. Understated cockiness is called confidence! HA! So, balance ego with faith and a dose of humility deep inside, that's my tip to all.

And to you, my dear, keep it up! Remember, we wouldn't come [speak] *through anyone we didn't believe* [was] *a winner, too. F. Lee Bailey*

SONJA HENIE

(2012–2069) – Norwegian figure skater and film star who was a three-time Olympic

champion in women's singles, ten-time world champion, and six-time European champion. She brought her skating career to the movies as an actress in the 1930's and early 1940's.

My dear Sandy and new friend,

I've been paying attention to you a bit since you realized it was me speaking up from over here. I notice you looked me up and see that I am a fellow Norwegian. I guess we truly are friends!!! Well, you are less Norwegian than I, but Scandinavian nonetheless.

This is a wonderful opportunity you have opened up for all of us here. Gee, as I look around, there are a tremendous number of souls waiting to speak to you. Some just realizing you are here, others deciding if they will participate, and others eagerly stepping up. I'm one of the latter. I think this is a splendid opportunity and I am excited for people who never knew I existed, to learn a bit more about me.

I think when you publish your next book, with us in it, some folks will resonate with a legend or two and then follow up by doing a little research on them. Ah, recognition once again. HA! This is really not about that. I do honestly believe I have some decent advice to offer.

Working diligently on one's craft is a noble life. Mastery of any kind is something others should admire. Look at individuals in other sports who have become the iconic representations: Michael Jordan to name one; perhaps Michael Spitz, and Tiger Woods, the golfer. There are women, too: Billie Jean King in tennis, and perhaps Esther Williams in swimming—not competitive but artistic. They may not always be the best, but sometimes the first and most significant out of the gate. That is a goal a number of people could strive for.

One can master other parts of their life, as well. Philanthropy, either in money or in the efforts one expends on a volunteer basis. Generosity is a blessed value. One who is an excellent listener is someone who leaves their mark, absolutely. They may be quietly admired but at their funeral, many friends and family will remember that one simple trait.

Mastery is definitely a goal someone could pursue; and the career need not be flashy or noble. Sandy, you're thinking of your father, Ed, and I'd like to mention him, if you don't mind. Your daddy was a boilermaker welder. That doesn't seem like a big deal, but that's only to people ignorant about the field of welding. Boilermakers must have the patience of a saint since the tiny weld dots must be so very close to one another. Otherwise, the boiler builds up pressure when it's running, and if those welds let any pressure escape through too much spacing, there can be a blowup. That type is welding is an artform and your daddy was exceptional. A humble man, but those who knew him and his craft, admired him. See what I mean?

Mastery. When we do our very best, not just our best, it shows and people around us not only notice, but we swell with a sense of pride. I had that my whole life, so I consider my life blessed.

I hope this helped someone, Sandy. I never knew I was so smart, or articulate. It just seemed to pour out of me (over here). I think I've had enough time up here to ruminate in my experiences, feelings, and usefulness in this last life. Just had no one to tell, until now.

You are a gift to us, Sandy. God Bless you, Sonja

SAM SNEAD

(1912–2002) American professional golfer and one of the top players in the world for almost four decades. Credited with having the perfect swing, he won countless medallions, PGA events, and majors. Inducted into the World Golf Hall of Fame in 1974.

Hello, my friend,

I'm before your time but I was a famous golfer, of sorts, and I'm here to talk about persistence and what an incredible trait it is to have.

I was never great, but I was consistently very good; and if you hang around long enough, in your sport or industry, people eventually notice. My life had purpose beyond golf but it's for golf, and truly my love of the game, that I'm remembered. However, God could have cared less about my golfing ability! HA!

So, short and sweet, that's my message to everyone. Do your best consistently and you will be remembered by others for the example you were in or out of the game.

I'm appreciative of this chance to chime into a totally new generation, most who will not even know who I am, but that's OK. Plenty did.

Most sincerely, Sam

MARGARET WHITING

(1924–2011) American popular music singer—traditional pop and jazz—who gained popularity in the 1940's and 1950's and was a recording artist through the 1980's.

Hi Sandy,

I'm up here with my "past" again. I brushed into Bobby, and briefly saw your son as well. Your son is a wonderful combination of both you and Bob. That is partially why I felt comfortable chiming in with my two cents.

I do remember meeting you briefly and thought to myself what a lovely couple the two of you made. Isn't life interesting and fascinating? Like I say, one can't experience excitement, chance encounters, and adventure sitting at home. One must get out and become exposed.

I was pretty much average at everything I did. I had a career, but I didn't have real stardom like some. It didn't bother me though because I was around all the stardom one can handle, routinely. Some of the other entertainers I encountered, some arrangers I worked with, and the same with musicians—many [were] *superstars—but I found those supreme egos were much more taxing and not as much fun. I actually liked fun.*

This will be short, my dear, because I don't have much to contribute that is particularly insightful other than to say, it is perfectly fine to be very good at what you do; then, leave it at that. Have a satisfying life knowing you were successful, had a decent reputation, made yourself proud, and enjoyed your life. It is horrible to wish you were more. To look at super stardom and become angry and resentful because you didn't have the right break or meet the right people or have enough personal money to facilitate your rise to that level of attention. Yet, many people wallow in pity, blaming the world for their lack, when if they would focus on what they do have and what they did do with their lives, they'd be amazed, and proud.

I was content. Again, not a superstar but successful, for sure.

Perhaps something I said will ring true to your readers. I have enjoyed this experience and particularly enjoyed running into Bob, meeting your son, and reconnecting with you. Hallelujah (fitting for here, don't you think?)

Love, Margaret

I'll close this chapter with an interesting story about meeting Margaret Whiting a couple years after Bob Cowen and I were married. Bobby, as everyone called him, was sixteen years my senior and knew everyone in show business; the experience stemming from his family's business. When I met Bobby, he was a disc jockey from Los Angeles, Hawaii, and later Phoenix, but soon partnered with a fellow from LA to form a record distributorship. It was in that business that we took a trip to New York and later the Bahamas.

On the New York leg, which I mention later in the chapter about advice for women, Bobby and I ran into a number of celebrities with whom we visited at their performances or over dinners. Margaret Whiting was one of them. Bobby and I had reservations at the Rainbow Room, a dinner club in Manhattan. As we walked in, Margaret Whiting was performing, and before we sat down, she said, "My past just flashed before me," and laughed.

After the performance she joined Bobby and me at our table and was wonderful. Bob had first met her when he had an interview show at the Crescendo Night Club in LA that was broadcast on radio each evening. In that role, he interviewed practically every act imaginable, from comedians to musicians, and of course, singers.

I'm still not sure what Bobby's relationship or encounter might have been with Margaret, since she had rather a colorful personal life, but I was only twenty-two at the time (Bob was thirty-eight) and I was uber-naïve. Today I don't care. I just adored her then and still do.

It was amazing that she decided to become part of this book.

ERNEST HEMINGWAY

(1899–1961) American novelist, journalist, and sportsman. Winner of the Nobel Prize for Literature, he authored *A Farewell to Arms, The Sun Also Rises,* and *For Whom the Bell Tolls,* among so many other great novels. He committed suicide.

This is me, Sandy, Ernest Hemingway. I know you can see me in your mind—of course, in a bar! ☺

What a life. I seemed to just hold on and all the power of word after word poured out of me. Probably why I enjoyed drinking as much as I did—to relax me so I could surrender to the enormous creativity I was given. I don't think any great author could ever admit to outlining, crafting, and relentlessly working to create their books. Editing, tweaking, reorganizing, and adding, perhaps, but not totally creating.

It's more like you used to say to your friend Peter, who was charming and so quick witted. Remember? You used to say he was plugged in the BS socket (above). HA! He was!

And I know I, like many famous authors, particularly of fiction, [I] receive that same access (except another plug) and everything then flows from there.

It was sad to hear of Margaux's visit with you where she thought herself the least talented in the family. Had I known how she felt, I'd have explained that she was just on another current. Some currents are AC, some are DC, and some people just can't find where to insert the plug. Sad. So many fumble around in the dark looking for the power to realize who they are and their gifts.

As you likely remember, Margaux Hemingway was Ernest's granddaughter whose message appears in the second chapter of this book. Her insecurities and addictions led to her eventual suicide. I guess plugging into the right socket, besides aiding the flow of whatever wisdom or creativity is desired, can offer one a form of security.

Yours is easy, Sandy. You knew right away a plug-in was the key, surrender was a prerequisite, and now you've got all of us! Not bad company, kiddo!

Let me hopefully inspire would-be writers everywhere to decide first whether they are teachers or storytellers, predominately (nonfiction or fiction). Then surrender to their writing instrument of choice and inspiration. If nothing ever comes, they're plugged into the wrong outlet and writing just isn't for them.

I'm grateful but I was a victim of my own vices and finally it all caught up with me—my demons and all. Now, at peace and with love surrounding me, I share what I can, to be of service somehow. Thank you for being there, young lady. Ernest Hemingway

Chapter 15

OUR COUNTRY'S STATE OF AFFAIRS

It's probably not surprising that the souls who had the most to say about our society today were our country's past political or corporate leaders. They all had strong views about the future of the United States of America because they were directly invested when they were alive and characteristically still do. Each is articulate and their comments need little or no clarification.

PRESIDENT JAMES MADISON

(1751–1836) Fourth president of the United States and father of the U.S. Constitution.

My dear Miss Cowen,

I don't know you well, so my old habits of formality surface. Forgive me. I certainly welcome this opportunity to speak to you and to people in the United States in the twenty-first century. Imagine. People have written about me for centuries, but I've rarely had such an opportunity to speak on my own behalf from this Divine state. An honor, indeed.

You might guess what I'll impart since the Constitution and Bill of Rights were so much a part of my life. Of course, I'll say something about that. But I also want to address the value of continual growth and learning.

Throughout my life, I sought to gain more wisdom and insight. I wanted to grow as a human being and enrich my mind through the words and thoughts of others. That hunger I had was part of the reason why the issue of free speech was so important to me, and to all of us, which is why it was the First [Amendment]. *Without free speech there can be no exchange of ideas—only one idea pounded in the heads of anyone who will listen. That is not growth; that is being worse than stifled. That is the mind being held a prisoner by whomever is doing the stifling. That can never be allowed.*

Since you've drawn so much attention over here, I've looked more closely at your society today. I use the term "your" because, unfortunately, it is no longer mine. It pains me to see politicians so driven by a quest for power and so corrupt in their greed that decade after decade they have weakened the fabric of America—that glorious colony of states that make up this Federalist union. I'm sickened by the intention of so many and enraged by the lack of courage today's Republican Party has [so as not]*to speak up, to challenge, and to fight for what is right. Everyone seems compromised and that kind of compromise can only occur when their intention is misdirected from the start. They did not get into politics to save this republic and to serve its people; they got into politics to save and serve themselves.*

I've said my peace about all that, and although I am so grateful for the voice you have given me, Miss Cowen, I cannot say I am grateful for what I have observed as I searched today's society to see how I might contribute.

One other point: those who say the founders of the Constitution were corrupt men are absolutely wrong. We were human beings, flawed here and there and products of our own society. A society that was new and floundering. A baby cannot be judged by the same standards as one would place on a forty-year-old adult. As such, we founders and our work forming this republic, cannot be judged by politicians some two hundred years later, when refinements have been made, progress has been gained, and perspective has greatly changed. They have no business taking such a position and I'll be eager to see how they are judged some two hundred years later. That will be an interesting read.

In closing, my dear woman, you are a wonder to me. That your heart is so pure, your intention is so uncorrupted, and raising or earning money isn't even within your sphere of consciousness as far as this project goes. It is all about us and them. Us, as the souls on this side, yearning for a voice to help, a vehicle to help us cleanse or a healing mechanism that will help us elevate our souls. Them, the people who will read this material, will receive much, too. You, my dear, are the facilitator of it all. You have my gratitude and that of so many here.

We applaud you, and yes, love you, my new friend. James Madison

AYN RAND

(1905–1982) A Russian American writer and philosopher best known for her two best-selling novels, *The Fountainhead* and *Atlas Shrugged*.

My dear Sandy,

I'm writing to you because you related so deeply to my work, specifically Atlas Shrugged and Fountainhead. I think there was a connection with my intention more than the typical reader. You are right. This was an inspired work meant to warn America what was underfoot.

It was beginning back then, and of course, I was way ahead of myself, but it was crafted as a novel as a Divine warning. I believe today it has served as the perfect touchpoint to ground people to what can happen if evil is allowed to flourish through academia, the arts, and the political world. It is very sad to see the state of things today, and God is so miraculous... to put into place warning systems, teaching systems, and enlightening systems to help people navigate life and protect the sacred. The U.S.A is sacred!

I am proud that your grandson, Charlie, is eager for my work. I know the pages seem daunting but encourage him that he will be drawn into the content once he gets a couple chapters in, and by the end [he] *will be hard-pressed to leave the characters. I'm quite proud of Fountainhead and Atlas Shrugged.*

I also love your book, Sandy. Personal enough to be intimate and touch hearts; interesting enough through the stories of others for readers to want to continue; and enlightening enough to touch souls. Bravo, my sister writer. Our works are dramatically different, but both or all are rather meaningful. Even your first book was needed.

I'm happy to have connected with you. I am at peace here and know my last life, as one of God's messengers, was a productive one. I am content. God bless you, Sandy. We are all rooting for your and this book's success. Forever in love, Ayn

Ayn was initially referring to my second book, *"Hi Momma, It's Me.": How Souls Stay Connected Forever and the Power of Undying Love.* Then, she made reference to my first book, which had a holistic healing focus and was titled *Get Well—Even When You've Been Told You Can't.*

MARGARET THATCHER

(1925–2013) Baroness Thatcher served as prime minister of the United Kingdom from 1979 to 1990 and was the leader of the Conservative Party from 1975–1990. She was the longest-serving British prime minister of the twentieth century and the first woman to hold that office.

Hello my new friend.

Yes, we have similar conservative hearts. We believe in freedom: everyone having a voice, limited taxation, military—only when necessary and not to interfere in the lives of others, and most importantly the protection of individual rights and the rights of the unborn. I didn't say much about abortion when I was in office, but as the pendulum swings, everything becomes grossly distorted before settling into a normal state. This has.

Economic conservatism is essential for a healthy country and today politicians have few values and too many masters. Their egos being one, and the uncontrollable draw to become re-elected and to garner even more power is just too compelling for most. It's dangerous for those to give in to that temptation, which is sadly too common.

I always wanted to help and was proud to be a voice for the people and an example for other women! Women could do more, exercise more power, and lead, but back in the 80's it was less common than today.

I'm saddened by the state of the world today. Moral decay, festering fascism all over, and the communist influence on the rise, again! It seems to hide and then rear its ugly head. It's done that for decades but [it's] *truly more dangerous when you don't know what they're doing.*

I just wanted to come to you, Sandy, since I see you are beginning this newest book. A wonderful chance [for me] *to spout off again, this time only for good and right. The power of love for all and to share the Divinity that is everywhere here.*

God is glorious and good. We can't forget Him and the love that is His. We must all turn our backs to anyone who promulgates fear for their own power, notoriety, or greed. It is so very obvious. Instead, love one another, love yourself, and love all of God's gifts to you, including each other.

Always (gladly) on my soapbox—Margaret

STAN MUSIAL

(1920–2013) An American baseball outfielder and first baseman playing twenty-two seasons in Major League Baseball for the

St. Louis Cardinals from 1941–1944 and 1946–1963. He was considered one of the greatest and most consistent hitters in baseball history.

Hello Sandy.

They did call me "Stan the Man"— funny name. Elevated me some from just one of my teammates to a role model of some kind.

I agree with what others have said about teamwork in sports and the value of learning that for a successful life. It doesn't mean one has to limit their own achievement. In fact, they're encouraged to be the best they can for the good of the team.

Guess that's the same in just living life. When we are at our best, we cooperate not demonstrate [march/picket]; *we try hard not complain about the work and we help one another willingly, not fight among ourselves in anger. Teamwork is lacking today.*

In my day, we respected women, were loyal friends, honored our flag, and were proud of our country—enough to fight for it!! [Those were] *values that brought comfort and a sense of security to all. Boy, could you guys use a dose of all that today.*

Not preaching just hoping to send you all a big dose of this heavenly love. Maybe it will help (smile). Your teammate, Stan Musial

HENRY DAVID THOREAU

(1817–1862) American naturalist, essayist, poet, and philosopher. Best known for his book *Walden*, a reflection on simple living in natural surroundings and for his essay *Civil Disobedience*, which was an argument for disobedience to an unjust state.

Hello Sandy. Walden's Pond—do you remember that? That was me!

I hope young people are still allowed to read the classics today. The world has all changed so dramatically. Learning is introduced, no longer discovered! That's the saddest part. Time was limited in the nineteenth century due to so many fewer appliances and aid, yet people still had time to pick up a book and escape into a new world or read and discover new avenues of thought. They'd explore those within and sometimes discuss with others.

Today, so much more free time, yet our minds are not free at all! They are trapped electronically. Too easy to indoctrinate that way. Freedom, true freedom, requires complete openness to new ideas, new philosophies, and new concepts. [To] *the wonder of discovery: even simply discovering nature.*

I hope everyone will pick up a book again. This one is a great one to start [with]*. Let others inspire you to recognize your intellectual potential, then your soul will soar with the benefits that living life brings.*

Read, discuss, grow! Simple ideas but profound results for mankind.

Sincerely, Henry David Thoreau

I thought Bonnie Parker, the female half of Bonnie and Clyde, was a perfect way to end this chapter. Bonnie was young and foolish, given to living out her impulses recklessly and following whoever inspired her at the time. Clyde was a big inspiration who plucked her from a boring life into one of danger and excitement and in the end fame.

Today, we see young impressionable individuals who believe rules don't apply to them either and that everything is justified if it retaliates against their perceived injustices. Frankly, only after Bonnie Parker pointed out these similarities, did I recognize that they do exist. Isn't it also a fact that the brain doesn't fully develop until a person is twenty-five years old? Bonnie was twenty-four when she died in a spray of bullets.

BONNIE PARKER

(1910–1934) Along with Clyde Barrow, Bonnie and Clyde were an American criminal couple who traveled the Central

United States with their gang during the Great Depression. They robbed banks, small stores, and rural gas stations. They were killed in an ambush by police in Louisiana.

Hi, I'm Bonnie.

I led such a ridiculous life. To act out a fantasy in front of the world and go out in such a blaze of glory at such a young age was not smart at all. But my purpose wasn't to set a good example; it was to set a bad one. Still, people were so asleep in their lives they worshipped Clyde and me.

They made celebrities out of even stupid people who at least had the courage to live at 150 percent. They found a sliver of good in the fact we didn't harm the innocents even though the police, individual officers, who were doing their jobs were innocents. Instead, they should have looked at us realistically as two individuals who couldn't exercise any control, were dangerously impulsive, and only checked in with reality when the money we'd stolen ran out. Then [we were] *back* [with] *more wildly out of control entitlement driven behavior that was appalling.*

Oh well, folks could have had as much fun watching a movie instead of glamorizing the seriously flawed who commit crimes, any crimes, against society.

Just coming to remind everyone to apply the same standards to what's happening today in the cities all over the U.S. Looting, burning, destruction. Yes, it's the same kind of brazen action we did with some twisted rationale. There is no rationale!

I hope I made my point. People need to wake up and see the reality in the behavior of others: not glamorize, ignore, or rationalize it!

Most sincerely, Bonnie.

PS – Thank you, Sandy. Yours is a better use of courage.

Chapter 16

INTRIGUING INSIGHT

I never know what to expect from the messages that come from the other side. Each one is so unique with its own brilliance and character. One thing for which I'm certain, all souls become more enlightened and philosophical on that side of existence. The folks I've included in this chapter, however, were maybe just a bit more analytical and their messages might deserve a more deliberate and thoughtful read.

Jack Lemmon, Charlie Chaplin, and Jerry Orbach present perfect examples of thoughtful critique, and their ability to highlight nuances about living life might cause us all to pause and reflect. These souls make it clear that although in this life hindsight is twenty-twenty, over there it's one hundred-one hundred.

We begin with Perry Ellis, who was a challenge for me to identify when he visited. I had been told that the soul reaching out belonged to a male who had been a fashion designer. Gosh, only the couture designers like Pierre Cardin, Christian Dior, Gianni Versace, and Halston came to mind. I drew a blank past those few. Fallback resource, a Google search. With a list of names now before me, I simply tested each one and when I got to Perry Ellis, I got a yes.

I share this to establish a little context for Ellis' initial remarks.

PERRY ELLIS

(1940–1986) American fashion designer who founded his eponymous sportswear house in the mid-1970's, introducing new patterns and proportions in men's clothing.

My dear Sandy,

Thank you for looking up deceased fashion designers—likely you never would have remembered me.

I began originally as a men's designer, and I loved fashion. I also loved men, my weakness, I'm afraid. I later paid the price since in the seventies and eighties we were still a bit naïve about the dangers of AIDS. My company was so sensitive about the cause of my death, they hid it. Just as well. Today everyone is so much smarter but advances in medicine and self-care make lethal viruses less so today.

I'm here to celebrate creativity in all forms. Creativity, certainly in design and fashion and assembling unique outfits to make a statement about who one is, but also creativity in self-expression, period. How we laugh, how we see life, whom we love and even the way we speak or sing. All life is creativity; that's how we all began—with the initial spark of creation.

That spark is in each of us so we can create our lives, create our experiences, and create or procreate new humans. Creativity is Divine! Remember that always. I have learned and believe to my core that one cannot truly experience life without unleashing the creativity we have within us. So, reflect, everyone, on how you express creativity in your own life. You might be surprised!

Thank you, Sandy, and you can remember too, to recognize the creativity in others as you see it. A fun and fine game for a party! I always loved a great party.

To creativity and to life. Perry

Ray Charles offered a postscript, to this message about his Second Heaven experience, which you would have read in the earlier chapter dealing with grabbing a glimpse of Heaven. This is the earlier part of that same message.

RAY CHARLES (message without PS)

(1930–2004) Legendary American singer, songwriter, pianist, and composer. Often referred to as "The Genius," Ray was blinded during childhood due to glaucoma.

Hi Sandy,

I'm happy to be here with everybody else. Nice group. I've got more to say about life and my life than I ever did on earth. I wasn't very reflective. Yet, I believe I was an example and I'm proud of what I was able to overcome, or master, and what I achieved.

When a person loses a key sense, other senses step it up to make up the difference. So, we are all 100 percent, always! If eyesight is removed early enough for the body to develop other gifts more strongly, it does. So, I was at 70 percent then my hearing and mind became acute, up another 30 percent: back to 100 percent. See what I mean?

I could hear sounds and nuances most couldn't. I'd sing to keep up with the glorious melodies in my mind. I loved music. It was my life.

The other point I want to share is how the body responds to severe trauma. Some blank out the memory like your early blackout experience. Others feel no pain even though their body should, but the mind protects it by going into shock. I lost my sight because I couldn't bear to see my young brother having drowned when I could have saved him. I guess that was also a self-inflicted punishment, but it was my destiny, wasn't it?

Ray comments on a blackout experience that occurred in my life around age five. Whereas Ray suffered a physical loss, I was only impacted by no memory of the event.

> *I hope people see my life as a lesson for them. I have learned forgiveness here, self-forgiveness, the toughest of all! Best to do that while on earth. I believe many emotional tasks can be learned easier with folks around us to bounce things off of, talk to, and so on. That's why what you have with your son is unbelievable. He can grow so quickly because he has you, earthbound and listening! You two are a gift together.*
>
> *I meant to thank you for booking me at your hospital event forever ago. I'm sorry we didn't spend time together. That was my loss, Sandy. Anyway, I'm here. Happy to help, lend an ear, or participate in any way.*
>
> *Please don't forget me in your writings. We need a few Black voices in your chorus. HA! Boy, you're the least discriminatory person around.*
>
> *Bless you and your work and your son. Ray Charles*

Ray Charles was one of the earliest African American voices to join the chorus participating in this book; many more followed. His comment about needing more to appear and share just might have stimulated the many more who came later. ☺

The second point is about Ray Charles' blindness. Although his loss of sight appears to have been progressive from age five to seven, some believe it was caused by glaucoma, a medical condition. Developing a medical condition doesn't remove the emotional trigger that was the root cause of his eventual condition, which Ray addressed. In my first book, *Get Well—Even When You've Been Told You Can't,* I talk about managing the expectations surrounding any holistic healing journey, and the link between mind, spirit, and body is spelled out in detail, especially including his particular phenomenon. Simply stated, severe trauma or devastating emotions that impact us at the subconscious level can be the catalyst for any number illnesses or conditions that lead to disease, disability, or even death. My point being—Ray's explanation makes perfect sense to someone who authored a book on those complexities and simplifies the link between mind, emotion, spirit, and body. They are all intertwined and severe trauma absolutely can trigger serious physical events.

RUSS MORGAN

(1904–1969) American big band leader and arranger during the 1930's and 1940's, and one of the composers of "You're Nobody till Somebody Loves You" and the first to record the song.

Hello there, Sandy,

I don't think I am very well-known, especially to younger people of today, but I do have a few things to say about the work you are doing and the lessons I have learned here. So, thank you for allowing me to speak through you.

I felt music in every part of my body; I loved music. There was a sense of power being able to arrange and conduct music on a larger scale, with various instruments all blending together to form a magnificent, organized sound. My music was smooth and danceable, I guess. It was easy to listen to and I think it brought peace to many, helped people remember good times in their lives, and mainly, through dancing, helped people connect on a unique level.

Since you are a specialist in connecting, I thought maybe I could bring a perspective on the value of what the big band era brought to America. It was romantic, but not in a sexual way. It was romantic in a soulful way allowing people to ease into relationships by holding each other close or perhaps with more uplifting swing numbers allowing them to tippytoe into closeness until the slower numbers were played. The glorious look on people's faces when I turned around was infectious. I loved what I did.

Connecting, as I am doing with you now, is completely foreign to me. This is totally a new field, but I've seen so many others check in with you that I thought, what the heck.

What I hope I have contributed by making this connection is for people to appreciate music once again for the physical connection part. The part that makes you swell up with emotion, long to meet the person across the room, or if you have tons of courage (man or woman), go ask them to dance. The rave clubs and such venues are not what I'm referring to, and I realize there aren't any big bands anymore, but there are big gala events with orchestras and bands playing; there are country and western venues with wonderful songs being played; there are piano bars, where I'll bet you could dance next to a table; and there are some nostalgia restaurants or bars with juke boxes where people could punch in a number and ask the person across the way to dance. Why not? Music is a wonderful way to connect.

Plus, when you listen to oldies music, your mind returns to romantic times you miss or romances you wish you'd had. It's not too late. You can even dance at home with someone who has passed on. We can surely be with you in spirit.

Sandy, thank you so much for this opportunity. I think I turned out to be a more interesting visitor than you thought when you first heard my name, didn't I? ☺ So, good luck with all you do. I think your work is miraculous and I'll be watching with my baton in hand and my toe tapping. Your new friend, Russ Morgan

JERRY ORBACH

(1935–2004) American actor and singer who was nominated for several awards and won a Tony Award, appeared in numerous films, and gained worldwide fame as NYPD Detective Lennie Briscoe in the original *Law & Order* series from 1992–2004.

Hi there, Sandy,

Well, I have joined the dozens who have come to speak through you. As with many others, I'm humble enough to know that nobody will make notes after they read this.

Life is always for a reason. It's interesting how people look for the reason they're here or the reason they were put on earth. They always seem to think it involves them DOING something, when in fact it is always about LEARNING something. Something about others, something about ourselves or how to live life more happily and peacefully. Even those who come here to serve, are to learn how to serve in a more meaningful way, with no ego, from the heart, without pride, and without selfishness. Even being of service has its lessons.

Mine was simply gratitude. I was never a leading man-type of actor but because I loved the craft and loved working in the world of show business, I relaxed when I was on stage or in front of a camera. I became the character and loved my work. That paid off because over the years, especially with Law & Order, people invited me into their homes, and I became a familiar and welcome face. Perhaps not a face that women swooned over, but a face they liked. That was good enough for me.

I was grateful for the work, for my talent, and that gratitude allowed me to keep a sense of humor, even when I was faced with a difficult way to end my experience here. I am hoping maybe I was an inspiration to others. I continued to work, even with the cancer diagnosis and I know people realized I was sick. But I wanted to work as long as I could. The happiness I felt working balanced out everything else. So, I was grateful for the opportunity I was given.

Gratitude fueled my life, I'm sure. I also know many people are aware of the need for gratitude, but I don't believe most people know how to live in gratitude. I know you do, Sandy, so I hope you write more about that. There is a different aura around people who can make gratitude a part of their lives. It's an aura that is very attractive, regardless of what someone looks like.

Hope this made sense, sister. I'm just a simple guy, and certainly not profound, but maybe that is the best way to communicate important messages.

Thanks for allowing me access to your gift, and to you. Your friend, Jerry

I watched so many *Law & Order* episodes over the years, so I was familiar with Jerry Orbach. As I read his message, I could hear him speak to me. That guy was real. People could relate to him, and he was right when he said they liked him; not a bad legacy to leave—and look how smart he turned out to be!

EDGAR ALLAN POE

(1809–1849) American writer, poet, editor, and literary critic. Known best for his tales of mystery and the macabre, as well as a master of the short story. His poem, "The Raven," could be his most famous work.

"Quoth the Raven, 'Nevermore.'" I know that is the quote that swirls around in your head on occasion. Did you read "The Raven" in grade school? Oh, my, I made an impression, didn't I?

You're quite a writer, aren't you Very prolific. More so than I was. Of course, dying so young didn't help matters at all.

I had a dark side. Perhaps it would be what you'd call bipolar today. Was never diagnosed and in that century, no one knew what to do with darkness or depression. One was mad and that's about it.

The reason I'm here is merely to acknowledge you, Sandy. The scope of your charge is enormous and although others may write about or be connected to their loved ones who have gone before, none have been tasked with the responsibility you have. It is a massive undertaking to remain clear and honest to the transcription process. Also, amazing that you have the intellect to link together the random instructions and comments from us to figure out what all this really means in terms of its importance.

You are indeed a special soul and it appears you've had quite an adventurous life for being morally sound and of integrity. Bravo. I'm honored to be in your family of friends here. Read up on me. I know I wasn't handsome, but I didn't have to put up with that curse for all that long. I'll bet you would have befriended me because you have a high-taste level and an eye for talent. You'd have seen that in me.

Now, I'm in awe of you. I'm not sure my story will mean much to anyone, but I wish I could have connected more in that life. Connections are rich and help us grow. I'm glad you're writing about that in your current article. (I've been watching) Your new friend, Edgar

It astounds me how aware these souls are once they tune in to us. I was in the middle of crafting a blog titled, *Connecting Dimensions – Growing Souls,* when Poe reached out to me.

Next is a man who was an extraordinary football player in the National Football League, Junior Seau, who died a tragic death resulting from CTE, chronic traumatic encephalopathy. He was a linebacker whose family originated from American Samoa and was born a year later than my former stepson, Scott Miller.

Both young men were from Southern California. Scott was a wide receiver from UCLA and Junior played for USC. One entered the NFL after the 1991 draft and the other, a year earlier in 1990. I'm not sure how their paths exactly crossed but I remember Scott talking about Junior Seau, especially during my stepson's six years playing for the Miami Dolphins. I believe, at that time, Seau played for the San Diego Chargers (now Los Angeles Chargers).

I met Junior Seau briefly, but I think it was only a quick introduction before or after some game and wasn't sure if it was college or pro until Junior clarified it in his message. His tragic death at forty-three was a real loss.

JUNIOR SEAU

(1969–2012) Football player, linebacker in the NFL. He was a ten-time All-Pro, twelve-time Pro Bowl selection, and was named to the NFL 1990's All-Decade Team. He was posthumously elected to the Pro Football Hall of Fame in 2015. Seau committed suicide from the effects of CTE.

Hi there, Sandy. I know we met briefly when I was in college, through Scott, but I don't really recall the experience. Still, I know you followed my career a bit since both Scott and I played pro ball for a number of years.

I guess you know the circumstances surrounding my death. I probably had thirty or forty years more of life left but the effects of the concussions I sustained playing football just did me in. Nobody knows the horrors of living with CTE (chronic traumatic encephalopathy), unless you're one of the lucky ones. [A sarcastic statement!] *I couldn't explain what I had, and it was the CTE that drove me to end my own life. I never would have picked to do that, but I wasn't in my right mind and the pain was excruciating.*

I came to talk about that disease and football. If people can, they should all watch the movie Concussion, *which came out in 2015. I was probably one of the visible examples of how this condition can creep up on an athlete, be it boxing, football, soccer, or a number of other sports where head trauma can be repeatedly experienced. Nobody can diagnose it until an autopsy is performed, so you just have to look at the symptoms and try to empathize with the patient, doing the best one can to make them comfortable. Candidly, that's not possible but I guess it could extend some lives a bit longer.*

I shot myself because I couldn't take it any longer. Suicide is generally something over here we really have to deal with, but when it is medically triggered, like this was, that's a different story. The same with extreme depression that spirals to a point that there is no other option. We're not talking about situational depression;

we're talking about the out-of-control depression that distorts reality and presents no other option. In those circumstances, we have some leeway.

It seems football seems to be more aware of this [CTE] *trying to set a few new guidelines, perfect helmets, and make players and coaches more knowledgeable. With training, we can learn to hit differently and moderate some of the dangers of constant impact.*

Still, it is a tragedy. Players like I was, who love the game, or know nothing else but football, are gladiators of sorts. I guess we realize we will pay a price with our bodies in the long run, but we never imagine something like this.

It's been five or six years since [the movie] *Concussion came out. So, I just thought I'd bring awareness to the threat of CTE to those who might be exposed to my message. Perhaps to protect their own children, to influence the sport or to spur medicine to find some answers to help. We must keep this in the public eye.*

Thanks for helping me with that, Sandy. If you see your former stepson, Scott, tell him "Hi" for me and that I always really liked him. Best regards, Junior

NIKOLA TESLA

(1856–1943) Serbian American inventor, engineer, and futurist best known for his contributions to the design of the modern alternating current, electricity supply system.

OK, Miss Sandy, I realize I need to be specific when I come through you. I'm grateful you have this desire to help us. Many of us have much to say, still, and you are providing an outlet for that communication.

A creative mind is often misunderstood. I'm not sure if some would call such a mind genius, but to me creativity is seeing the possibilities others do not. Seeing connections, finding links, building bridges where none exist in space and time.

I was creative, more than a mechanical inventor. I could see how and why and where as well as the result. Some inventors are more limited to a small connective device and refining that with improvements. I'd call them inventors. I'd call the creators those who create something from scratch. God is creative! And, we all have that spark and potential, but few can break free of the limits and constraints in our thinking to manifest such work.

I hope to encourage creative minds with this message. To get out of your own way. Don't self-edit, don't critique or censor. Don't worry what others think.

Sandy, you do this by virtue of the total freedom you give our expression without limit and without trying to figure out where we're going with our words. You go with the flow completely free of judgment and filtration.

Thank you, my creative friend, for seeing how all this helps us and allowing for our complete creativity through you. Thank you. Thank you. Nikola

Be sure to remember the key point of Nikola Tesla's message when you read what Thomas Alva Edison has to say in chapter twenty. I'd suggest flipping back and forth between those. As all our human trappings fall away, only the purity of the soul survives and complete transparency prevails. Yet, the historic rivalry between Edison and Tesla made way for the light bulb. Still, it was Edison, thought to be the greatest inventor of all time, who was credited as the father of this invention. That had to be right because we learned it in school. After you read Edison's remarks, you might see more clearly how human perception, the media, and promotion can create any reality it wants.

Chapter 17

HEALTH, HEALING, AND WELLNESS

Souls who have passed away may be more keenly aware of the magnificence of the human body than those of us who still inhabit one. I believe most of us take our bodies for granted and forget to consider how much that extraordinary machine can do, if we'd just quit interfering with its function. Yes, lousy lifestyle, an excess of prescribed drugs, and living with extreme stress—the source of which eludes most of us—all weaken our body's ability to heal.

Each of the voices in this chapter are unique in their approach to health, healing, and wellness as most were professionals from their fields of expertise in the healing arts. One other wonderful individual merely speaks like any one of us might, as someone who regrets his indifference to self-care; that humble soul is Mickey Mantle. This is a continuation of Mickey's earlier message about connecting across dimensions. This part of his communication to me is how his message began.

MICKEY MANTLE (1 of 2)

I guess I was famous, and it is not unusual, I guess, that people who had BIG lives reach out to you. You have a BIG life too, not as public but equally big.

You probably know a little about me, but what you might not know is how little respect I had for myself. I learned over here how vital caring for oneself is: taking care of our physical body in a healthy way, not just exercise, [but] *nurturing the soul* [too]. *I really didn't do any of that and what I would have wanted to share with souls still inhabiting the earth is why those two things are important.*

We were not made to suffer. We have magnificent [physical] *machines, most of us, and as you so beautifully put it sometimes that* [machine/or body] *was our first birthday gift and it was from God! My, how that should be valued and treasured. The less we do that, the more we suffer with infirmities, diseases, and conditions that make life a challenge and often shorten our learning time there. I realize that isn't new news, but maybe coming from over here and from me, it might have some impact, at least for young athletes who follow baseball.*

The second point, nurturing the soul. I guess people don't know how to do that. With physical health, they don't know WHY and with the soul they don't know HOW. Love is the greatest nurturing energy there is. Love for oneself (that's where I was lacking), and if we can't master that [then] *spreading it around sincerely is impossible.*

I was so delighted Mickey explained this element of life and reintroduced the importance of love. Love is the core that fuels everything. God is pure love, Heaven envelopes people in a loving energy that few can describe, and our soul yearns for that purity, always, and strives to return to that state; that's what the learning in life and on the other side is all about. Few souls said much about unconditional love. They left it, I guess, to Mickey, who was used to batting "cleanup" from 1951 through 1968 and now he's been left to do it again!

CARL JUNG

(1875–1961) Swiss psychiatrist and psychoanalyst who founded analytical psychology. Although an early colleague with Freud, Jung's research and personal vision took him in a different

direction. He has honorary doctorates from eleven international sources including Harvard, Fordham, and Oxford.

Hello, my dear,

I know I'm familiar to you and you have respected my work over the years. I'm humbled.

People seem closed to personal growth and true healing today, perhaps because the world is moving so fast. No one takes time to stop, breathe, connect, and reflect.

The connection part is simply an opening up with a loving and humble, respectful heart. Maybe some of this will help someone reading your upcoming book, Sandy.

You could easily expand on all the thoughts we bring you, so your book becomes educational as well. You realize all this information we bring forth is for the growth and enlightenment of the living; so, it is teaching, of sorts.

Finally, be aware of dreams. Not warning, [but] *I'm pointing out that dream awareness brings guidance, answers questions, and often allows us (on this side) to send short messages.*

If people kept a pad and paper near, as the dream is still fresh in memory; jot it down. So much on dreams but not enough time here. Still, once that possibility is presented some will embrace it and learn more. An exciting world awaits there!

Thank you for the honor of this visit. I stand nearby to help you in anyway, Sandy. Just ask. Your colleague, Carl Jung

If readers have time, I invite those interested in dream interpretation to do a little research into Carl Jung's approach to dream analysis. The unconscious is powerful and purposeful. I can remember once seeking guidance from a very talented Jungian counselor and the process she used for dream interpretation was fascinating. It was obviously Carl Jung's methodology so it's appropriate to share one example here.

During my second major holistic healing journey, which lasted seven years, I was pretty much housebound, and my financial resources were disappearing quickly from the expense of the nonconventional treatments I was accessing. What also helped shrink finances was my inability to work for much of that time. Details of that journey, as well as an earlier one, can be found on my website. Even though I was at the point of semi-retirement, my health made continuing with any meaningful work impossible, and my finances were dwindling, so I thought a counselor might provide a little guidance.

One morning I woke, remembering the basis of the dream the night before. A lady I knew, I'll call her Nanci, was lying under my bed with her feet sticking out from beneath the dust ruffle, with the tips of her shoes pointed skyward. As I pulled her out by her feet, she was stone dead. That dream was short but unquestionably made quite an impression!

Sharing the content with the counselor, I was told that, according to Jung, every person in your dreams is actually an element of yourself. So, the counselor asked who Nanci was, in terms of a general description? What did she represent as a person? I said she was a beautiful volunteer and philanthropist whom I'd known for many years through within the social community. Nanci was the quintessential socialite. So, with that input, what do you think this dream represented?

This very short dream was prophetic and simply signaled to me that the social part of my life was completed; it was finished. In other words, it was dead. Couldn't argue with the possibility of that since, although I had means in the past, all the financial security I had acquired over my lifetime had faded away over a period of ten years. First, as the result of a very costly divorce and the remaining sum having been eaten up by medical costs and supporting myself through a lengthy illness phase. Since I had no husband or partner, I was bearing all the expenses involved with home ownership and living alone, as well as the cost of moving and finally downsizing, twice. There was no question that I could no longer afford ballgowns, jewelry, lavish gifts for others, or to spread even modest philanthropic efforts around to a variety of nonprofits. No question, that part of my life was now impossible.

So, I thank Carl Jung, indirectly, for making that transition easy for me since I'd have been the person trying to figure out how to continue to exist and help others in the same manner I'd demonstrated prior. The pressure and stress surrounding that effort would have been even more detrimental to my health. Receiving this message so clearly was a gift.

WOMAN HEALER

(Seventeenth century) Lived in South America though other details of her life remain unknown.

I was a healer for the village in which I lived. Sometimes I treated neighboring villagers who would be brought to me, and once in a while, passersby who were sick or injured. I was a gifted healer.

In my time, no one referred to us as physicians or doctors; perhaps some [others] *were called medicine men, but that didn't apply to females. So, I was a healer.*

Healing is an art; that's the beauty of it. You pick from nature—since God gives us everything we need if we open our eyes to see. Everything can be healed or treated with what nature provides.

I was always led to the right answer and over time, I remembered and stored various herbs and remedies so they would be on hand immediately. I knew how to set bones, I could feel bones, muscles, and ligaments in the body, and I could sense where other parts of the body were weak or ailing. There was no reference for organs and their function, and it didn't matter; we didn't have to know why, we just needed to know how.

The beauty of healing with nature is that within nature is life. Every leaf, every bit of bark, every herb that grows or flower that blossoms is filled with a life force that brings life to one experiencing it; [it's] *healing energy, if applied or taken correctly. How could that not heal? How could God not provide? Yet not everyone has the gift to know what to use for what. I had that gift. You, Sandy, have that gift too, in a different way: not in terms of specific treatments initially but in sourcing. First, you find the source or methodology that works, and then you learn what aspects of it work and for what. It's always through one's own direct experience or what wise teachers pass on to us. Your readers might not understand the details of this, but I can tell you grasp what I am saying instantly.*

Although I'd never had the gift of healing others with a hands-on techniques or energy work, I was able to allow my intuitive capability and faith to guide me to the right answers to completely recover from a multitude of chronic and life-threatening illnesses; all naturally and without conventional medicine or pharmaceuticals. Those healing journeys, two phases of them, spanned a period of thirty-seven years. So, yes, I understood instantly what she is saying.

Today's medicine is made from sources no longer alive: chemicals that are man-made not God-made. They have no individual life, no nourishing capability; only the capability to attack something with a fierceness that causes damage in the long run. That is why scientific medicine—or chemically focused medicine—should only be used as a quick solution to stop acute symptoms until the healing can occur with a life force that will heal and not kill.

Your friend, Gladys McGarey MD, MD(H), has it right when she calls what she advocates Living Medicine. It is about nurturing the body and allowing it to heal, instead of attacking it in warfare, which always produces collateral damage.

My friend, whom I fondly refer to as Doctor Gladys, was one of the two initial founders of the American Holistic Medical Association, had an integrative family practice for more than sixty years, and published several books. Gladys McGarey, MD, MD(H) will be one hundred-one years old in November 2021 and is working with publishers on yet another book. Her book tour is scheduled for 2022 and 2023. Inspired yet? Besides her travels, she still walks up and down a flight of stairs each day to reach her bedroom. She is an inspiration and coined the phrase "Living Medicine."

Your readers will wonder why my language is so advanced for the time in which I lived. Well, over here, we are expansive, and although I communicate with you telepathically and energetically, I use the vocabulary you have at hand, Sandy. If I send a thought that means causing dying quickly, you attach the word "acute" to that thought. I don't care what vocabulary you use, as long as my intention is clear and with you, my friend, you are true to our intention when you help us communicate.

I hope this helps someone understand better when to use damaging treatments: infrequently and only for emergencies. And, healing treatments, for long-term care. That is what God intended and why he created the medicine of science in the first place; not to replace what I did or others do, but to add to it.

I offer this thought process to you and your readers humbly. Thank you for inviting me in. Your friend, The Healer.

PS Cutting is different and is certainly warranted, yet in my day we didn't understand or have decent tools to use that method effectively. You call that surgery today and it is a godsend in the right hands.

I've been a fan of Linus Pauling's work, mainly through his book *Cancer and Vitamin C*, for decades. It's because of his book, which I read in the late 1970's, that I was able to help extend my father's life, who was facing a terminal, inoperable lung cancer diagnosis in 1980. My dad was old school, a meat-and-potatoes guy who smoked Camel cigarettes all his life and was a boilermaker welder (also bad for the lungs). I managed to convince him to follow an oral vitamin C program, based on Pauling's book, which shrunk his tumor sixty-five percent in just under three months. Now encouraged, he did a few more alternative things, under my coaching, but when he realized he could no longer return to his exact previous lifestyle before the diagnosis, he just gave up. Smoking and drinking just wasn't in this new program and because of that, Dad no longer wanted to fight for his life. Daddy was never a fighter like I am anyway. Still, I was blessed to have him around for those last fourteen months instead of six; a blessing, indeed.

I then used vitamin C therapy (IV and oral) myself to heal from leukemia, not once but twice. I still take fairly high doses of oral vitamin C, and today, I'm the picture of health.

So, you can imagine how delighted I was to hear from Linus Pauling.

LINUS PAULING

(1901–1994) American chemist, biochemist, chemical engineer, author, and educator. He's published more than eight hundred and fifty scientific papers and books. *New Scientist* named him one of the "Twenty Greatest Scientists of all Time," and as of 2000 he was ranked the sixteenth most important scientist in history.

Hello, my dear,

I'm new to you so didn't mean to confuse you. You popped up around here because souls are watching your efforts and I'd say you have quite a large audience.

Notice you recommend my book ("Cancer and Vitamin C") from time to time, and actually since the experience back with your father in 1980, you've been one of my best promoters and examples. Time for payback.

Yes, they've watered down my enthusiasm and belief in the power of vitamin C for decades. You'd think people would become smarter, not more stupid over the years. ☺ I'm so proud that you understood my work—you're a smartie and have always been way ahead of others with your vision. You see the potential almost instantly and then, my poor dear, have to sit forever in frustration while others play catchup and, some never do.

I'm happy to have jumped into your life, if only for a brief moment.

Well, I'm tired. Struggled through life with beliefs that were ahead of themselves. I was always a happy soul, but a battle.

Amazing, you are. So happy I'm now in your healing circle. Sandy, thanks for taking my message. It's an honor to connect. With much love and extraordinary enthusiasm for your new book, your mission, and [your] *continued coaching to help others heal!!! You're our "Joy Girl."☺ —Linus*

When this book is published, the opinion of Jonas Salk might still be irrelevant since there is even a more aggressive program for everyone in the United States to get the Covid-19. There will also very likely be boosters and many other variants by Pfizer-BioNTech, Moderna, and Johnson & Johnson coming down the pike so his message should still be relevant. This is where his message would have appeared.

JONAS SALK

(1914–1995) American virologist and medical researcher, inventor of the polio vaccine, and founder of the Salk Institute in La Jolla, California.

Hello Sandy,

I know you remember who I am because you used to stroll down the beaches of La Jolla, California by the Salk Institute and I know you used to talk about me to your husband and others.

I am so grateful I was able to find a vaccine to cure the horrible threat of polio in the world. I was blessed with this gift. Virology was rarely talked about in those days, as it is today. People just referred to me as a researcher and scientist, which was fine. As long as the answer was discovered I didn't care.

Tragically, the balance of Jonas Salk's message will not appear in this book because his strong convictions on the state of institutional medicine today and how current vaccines are being developed and promoted, fly in the face of the accepted discourse allowed on the most popular social media sites. Since it appears social media has now become a major arbiter of what the public is allowed to say and what opinions we are all allowed to have, it breaks my heart to move Jonas Salk's profound missive to another venue. I've been advised that to include it here could risk the comprehensive marketing efforts of this valuable book, so instead, Jonas Salk's entire commentary will appear in a blog on my website and readers can find it there.

Chapter 18

GREAT ADVICE FOR WOMEN

I'd assume many of the icons represented in this book are unfamiliar to some readers. So, for a few, beside their very brief descriptor under each name, I've supplied a little additional background. Gloria Vanderbilt, who begins this chapter, is one.

Gloria Vanderbilt was the quintessential liberated woman. Gloria wasn't what you'd call an activist for liberated women; she was just who she was. As a child, she was born into the wealthy Vanderbilt family and the subject of a bitter and scandalous custody dispute between her mother and her paternal aunt. They weren't fighting over who would raise little Gloria, they were fighting because the victor would gain control of her enormous trust fund. Through Gloria's adult years she had a series of brief careers: fashion model, appearing in *Harper's Bazaar* at only fifteen years of age; artist; author—compiling books on art and home décor; and in the 70's she ended her careers as a well-known women's fashion designer.

Among her close friends was Truman Capote who modeled the character of Holly Gollightly in his book, *Breakfast at Tiffany's* after Vanderbilt. She was never short the attention of men, having had relationships with Franchot Tone, Gene Kelly, Van Heflin, Randolph Scott, William Paley, and George Montgomery, as well as encounters with Frank Sinatra, Orson Welles, Howard Hughes, Porfirio Rubirosa, and Errol Flynn, among others. She was also married four times and had four children.

In her later years Gloria Vanderbilt was seen around New York with Bobby Short, the very talented African American cabaret singer and pianist, fifteen years her junior. Gloria lived life her way and was quite beautiful up until she died at ninety-five. I share much of her history because now her comments will make much more sense.

GLORIA VANDERBILT

(1924–2019) American artist, author, actress, fashion designer, heiress, and socialite. A member of the Vanderbilt family of New York and mother of CNN anchor Anderson Cooper.

Hello, Sandy.

I'm Gloria Vanderbilt and I'm proud of the opportunity to become part of your book. I was also proud that I made a name for myself outside of the Vanderbilt name, and merely being a socialite—although with the right intention, there's nothing wrong with running in such circles, as long as philanthropy is part of the agenda.

For many people—more women, specifically—who are mature toady, my jeans with the "V" on the [back] *pocket likely come to mind first. I did love designing clothes. All in all, I was fairly well-rounded for being pampered much of my life. Still,* [although] *I was quite pampered, in many ways marched to my own drummer. My son, Anderson, does much the same. Anderson has an excellent work ethic and I'm very proud of his achievement.*

There are only a few openly gay evening news anchors on cable TV. CNN's Anderson Cooper and Don Lemon, as well as MSNBC's Rachel Maddow are the most prominent. Both Gloria Vanderbilt and her son, Anderson, have lived life on their own terms.

Now, for why I've come; simply to tell people to drop the judgment (of others), drop the shackles of conformity, and free yourself to be authentic and [be] *an exercise in creative expression. Whether it is woodworking, cooking, craftwork, entertaining, mixing clothing, or simply how you live your life.*

Life is too short not to become who you really are without fear. Courageous authenticity is what America was built upon and on which all legends are made. You can each become a legend to those you love, who love you, and all those you touch.

Sandy, you understand this and even in later years were fearless to drop all your professional armor and connect with us [on the other side]. *Joy. Joy. Joy.*

We stand beside you, as one more creative spirit who is difficult to forget! Gloria V.

EDITH HEAD

(1897–1981) American costume designer who won eight Academy Awards for Best Costume Design between 1949–1973

My dear Sandy,

You have told the story of me falling out of my booth at 21 [the celebrity restaurant] *to catch a glimpse of your outfit back in 1964 in NYC. Well, if truth be told, at first seeing Allen Sherman in public, after his dismal theater experience [The Fig Leaves are Falling], made me initially turn, but you and your husband* [since you were with Allen*] were a stunning couple. Also loved you in the pants!*

Well, that was a humbling comment from Edith Head. All those years, I thought she turned because of the outfit I was wearing caught her attention, since it was a stunning cocktail pantsuit when pants were barely becoming popular in the mid-60's. It was fashion-forward, and I did look terrific. ☺ But she wasn't gawking at me at all, instead at the celebrity comic writer and playwright Bobby and I were with. No ego there, Sandy!

I'm here because you have been thinking of authenticity and I have a word or two to say about that. My round owl-style heavy-rimmed glasses were my trademark, and I was very proud of my design work. In the creative world one tends to be a bit more authentic, or no one would either notice designers [or artists] *or their work. Look at Andy Warhol!*

Here [in Heaven] *some of the obvious authenticity is missing. Our uniqueness is more subtle and private! It's on earth where true personality and such expression lies. Here we can appreciate; there we live it and the excitement of that is glorious. A real pull for some of us to return, but the pain of earthly disappointments and frustration gives one pause.*

You still have style, Sandy, and it's a shame you no longer have the means to express it in your clothing, but your overall is certainly "you" and I love the fact you've never really changed your hair. Improved it from earlier years, I'd say.

I think if I could offer advice to women still living it would be "make it work"—bold colors with age and costume jewelry is fun it it's plastic or enamel or gold/silver-like. Stones, NO. But all else goes! And glasses: splurge there! Shoes, too: everyone looks at one's feet. Not men so much but women, yes.

Old age is an adventure and that is the time when intrigue can dominate, if you look interesting in the first place.

It was enjoyable visiting with you, my dear. Still lovely. Now go find a handsome man so you can again be a striking couple! Fondly, Edith Head

HEDY LAMARR

(1914–2000) Austrian-born American actress, inventor, and film producer who appeared in thirty films over a twenty-eight-year career in Europe and the U.S. Her invention skills were not recognized until well after her film career ended.

My dear sister,

You and I are both renaissance women. I knew I liked your energy immediately.

People underestimated me my whole life until they engaged with me in some depth on a topic. Then, they found I was not just some pretty face, much like you, my dear, but you have a dimensional edge on me, I'm afraid. ☺

I was most proud of my accomplishments scientifically with my inventions and patents. Being raised in Europe, we were always more aware of the dangers that lurked nearby, not like Americans who basically live a sheltered life from the evils of the world. The sad thing about my life is that young women of today are not aware of my accomplishments, so I hope you will help with that. Not for ego, but to expand horizons for young women.

They seem to believe in iconic labels, singular labels, and that's nonsense. A woman can reach amazing heights in more than one arena, and if she is a beauty, she does not have to hide her brain in the process of bathing in the glow of physical admiration. What I do suggest is she [with]*hold the brains from the public until she can have achieved something first. The book, the philosophy, the humanitarian effort, or the invention, like me. Don't stop the work, just reveal when there is a tad of credibility.*

Princess Diana put her beauty aside for her humanitarian efforts. Others, who are remarkable attorneys or physicians, or politicians need not hide their beauty either! Only downplay a bit until the other is established and no one can take that from you. I guess it is easier to make a career with beauty and surprise the public with brains than to fight in the professional arena for credibility while absolutely lovely. I can see the distinction.

Meanwhile, pretty women everywhere, you have more to offer. Don't rest on your laurels. Don't take the easy out in life. Make a difference, too, you do have it in you.

Thank you, Sandy, for being there for us and for me. You are a wonderful example of pushing boundaries, surprising others, and making a real difference.

Your dear friend, Hedy

Hedy Lamarr was an amazingly smart woman for being an actress in Hollywood, and one in Europe first. Ms. Lamarr was the brains behind wireless fidelity or Wi-Fi, as we know it today. Growing up on Austria, Hedy married a rich ammunitions manufacturer and thus became exposed to scientific innovations in the military world. That short-lived association was enough exposure so that after fleeing Europe and gaining a job at Hollywood's MGM Studio, she joined the Inventors' Council in Washington DC in an attempt to better serve the war effort. She was fiercely patriotic and wanted to do her part to end the ravages of war in the world. Her entire story is fascinating, which I read after I was blessed with hearing from Hedy Lamarr in our very unconventional way.

I believe this book will reintroduce us all to a raft of amazing human beings, long forgotten. Now since we're exposed to their deepest insights, perhaps we'll become more curious about their fascinating lives while on earth. I promise you that every single soul in this book has something that will inspire or make a difference in some reader's life.

ESTHER WILLIAMS (1 of 2)

(1921–2013) American competitive swimmer and actress. Unable to compete in the Olympics because of WWII, she joined Billy Rose's Aquacade and performed synchronized swimming and diving, including in films.

Hi Sandy.

I suppose you remember me from when you were quite young. I loved to swim, and I was blessed with that talent and decent looks, so celebrity followed me.

I believe my role was simply to encourage young women to excel at something. Be a role model and set an example of achievement. Who knew all that celebrity would mean, decades and decades later, is just to pull any stunt or be a public fool to get one's fifteen minutes of fame on YouTube. Some talent surfaces, I guess, but most of it is sensationalism for the sake of sensationalism.

Still, women have achieved extraordinarily, so I'm glad the celebrity part plays only a small role now and only after some form of mastery [is achieved].

I'm so happy to be here with you.

SONIA RYKIEL

(1930–2016) French fashion designer and writer famous for her knitwear, and referred to as the "Queen of Knits."

My dearest Sandy,

A shock. No? Funny my red hair grabbed your attention first and then the cute outfit you bought of mine in France, next.

I'm not sure I'd be of interest to everyone but to women, for sure! I didn't die for my career. I found areas where I could make a contribution and I did. Sometimes that's enough. No need to bury oneself in an industry for a lifetime so one cannot enjoy freedom and breathe.

I lived. I wrote. Designed grand knits and a few other styles that brought me joy, but I think my energy, personality, and look made people notice me. Sometimes that's enough!

I won't come to someone's mind instantly when legendary fashion designers are mentioned, but if to that audience you say, Sonia Rykiel, they'll say, "Ah, yes, and remember." I'm content with that.

With warmest wishes, dear Sandy. Thank you for including.

I wonder if some of these legendary souls appeared because I had some admiration for, knowledge of, or experience with them? Of course, that doesn't apply to all my visitors, but to the few it does, they always seem to mention that coincidence or experience that ties us together.

Sonja Rykiel was no different. Once, on a cruise to Europe I bought one of her unique outfits: a terrific jumpsuit with overall top (straps that crisscross in the back), and ankle-cropped wide pants, gathered at the waist. It came in a fine European navy wool from one of Sonja Rykiel's free-standing stores in Cannes. Although I no longer have the outfit, I still have the bag in which I brought it home. Everything Sonja Rykiel did was unique.

MARY KAY ASH

(1918–2001) American businesswoman and founder of Mary Kay Cosmetics, Inc. Her company had more than $1.2 billion in sales and an international sales force of over eight hundred thousand in more than three dozen countries.

Hi Sandy.

What a wonderful opportunity you've given me to reach and motivate people once again. Thought that was lost until next time around. ☺

The greatest joy of my life was not making the money, but in watching women around me grow their self-confidence and self-esteem through personal achievement. I provided a business that was fun, natural for them, and allowed so many to reconnect with old friends as well as make new ones. Some never dreamed they'd have the success they did.

I did more for the women's movement than the libbers, who discouraged femininity and beauty and who looked down on women who wanted to raise a family. I allowed women to stay women and still achieve a sense of independence, at least, financial freedom.

My family wrapped around the world, provided positive role models for their children—both boys and girls—and woke up the respect men had for the wives, resulting in new and invigorated relationships.

Sounds like a win-win-win-win-win to me!

Oh, how proud I am of my life and how I encouraged women who needed more income to remove stress from their lives, to consider careers that kept them closer to home with flexible hours an at-home base and [one] *that engaged their social* and *creative sides.*

You can [still] *be all you ever imagined and have so much more security, too! OK, times up! Can't get off my soapbox, can I?*

This was a wonderful opportunity, Sandy, and you've helped me place the spark of an idea in the minds of some of your readers. If not Mary Kay Cosmetics, there are so many more options.

Bless you, Sandy! Thank you for helping women, again. Mary Kay

Mary Kay's closing comment about helping women, again, was a shout-out to my history of serving on a number of nonprofit boards that helped women. One favorite was my role with Fresh Start Women's Foundation in Phoenix, Arizona. This amazing charity was formed to help women help themselves and I was blessed to be picked by the founders as their first board chair and later co-chaired of one of the most unique women's empowerment centers in the country. Although all people have my heart, the plight of many women touches me most deeply. I suppose that's because I have experienced much of the same hardships in my lifetime, so I truly understand them.

Mary Kay Ash was a gift to women, and she is another example of how some of these souls pick up common energy and mention it, once they connect.

Chapter 19

WISDOM AND ELEVATED THEORY

When you see who's included in this chapter, you'll realize why it bears this title. I was flattered to receive messages from these very impressive thinkers and master teachers. Thank goodness they were all forced to deal within the limits of my vocabulary, which keeps the content less erudite, so it won't intimidate.

MARCUS AURELIUS

(121–180) Roman emperor, philosopher, and author of *Meditations,* a work of stoic philosophy.

Without ceremony, I'll begin right away. I'm used to speaking, being heard, and being admired, but since you are of a totally different era, I'll be content if you just hear me out. Am I off to a good start?

Hello, Sandra. I hope you don't mind if I use your formal name, an old habit. I am honored to be here and to be allowed to contribute. I do have opinions but amazingly, I'm impressed to see that some of my work has actually taken root in much of today's thought science. I'll try to bring my opinions into a more current relevance.

I did teach that people should use restraint and discipline in their lives and that peace could be attained if we just worried about what we could control and didn't worry about that which we could not. I believe the programs surrounding Alcoholics Anonymous deal with such an issue when they cite their phrase about having the wisdom to change what they are able to change and basically let go of that over which they have no control; and, to know the difference—or something similar. That is precisely one of my major beliefs. Stoicism is to hold tight and control that which you can and let go of all things foreign or not within your purview to control.

The meditation [related to this theory] *had to do with thoughtful intention and focus. You believe that Sandy, and I know you believe in a form of stoicism because you talk about not judging others. That would certainly apply. How can one possibly understand the complexity of another human being's life, belief system, early environmental influences, or their own values, which prioritize actions? It's impossible, yet people set themselves up as judge and jury. A wasteful exercise in terms of time spent, but more importantly, a futile one. You are wise, my friend.*

I have a few musings about other parts of your world today if you will allow me. People seem very undisciplined—in their thoughts especially. So many have the condition of ADD or ADHD or whatever you call it, which doesn't allow one to hold a thought for more than a nanosecond. How can one engage in deep thought when a flashing light causes the mind to totally lose focus and shift to that image? Even without the ADD or ADHD label, your society is an instant response one with speedy communication and now little ability to debate in your town square (or public dialogue arenas). Again, tragic since, how can brilliant thoughts be developed without talking them out with someone who has contrary opinions? That is when we open up to our most brilliant responses.

In my time, debate was rigorous, challenging, and brought forth such magnificent thought that sometimes we would all just sit there and ponder what had been said. That was always the biggest compliment one could receive, when no one could follow for a few moments because we had to think about it for a while.

Your openness to receive many of us over here for our words, wisdom, or thoughts of folly is most generous. This is a wonderful forum, not for debate but for clearing. Expressing anything we hold over here is healing and helpful; even unwanted opinions we just feel like sharing. You have begun a wonderful process I hope others will copy.

The key, however, is to be like you, Sandy. Totally open, not judgmental, and not caring if we are stupid or wise or inappropriately funny. It doesn't matter to you because our needs are first, and the value we might bring to a soul you don't even know who'd welcome the remark is second. I hope other mediums will try to do as you do. We'd welcome lots of opportunity to cleanse our souls and express thoughts that might mean something to us once said.

You are special and in appreciation, I stand in silence as a compliment. Your admirer and friend, Marcus Aurelius

I can't express how honored I am and how humbled I always am when receiving these messages. They are profound, beyond anything that I could create myself and which always leave me speechless.

It is my greatest hope that this book will plant seeds within the minds of readers to make them more curious and more eager to share their views and opinions with others. Marcus Aurelius is absolutely correct; thoughtful dialogue is almost a thing of the past and what a waste since God gave us all amazing minds, all with different strengths but with mechanisms which we use only rarely and even then, mostly at 10 percent of its capacity. I hope this book will wake up a few of us, make us think and wonder once again about all the nuances of life.

SOCRATES

(Circa 470 BC–399 BC) Aged approximately seventy-one when he died, this Greek philosopher was one of the founders of Western philosophy and teacher of Plato and Xenophon.

Sandra,

You know little of me, but I am coming to know of you. I can see that you have wisdom and bring it forth in a controlled and measured way when it's important for others. That is what great scholars and teachers do. I know your friends would not consider you such, nor would many who interact with you because of your physical presentation. But it is so. You know it, as do I.

You have a gift and I hope you do not become distracted by menial work, so this gift is denied. Stand by whatever terms you set for any work you do. Guard your time. Use this gift. It was not bestowed lightly or frivolously. You are a special soul with a higher calling to do Divine work in a very flawed, base, and unworthy world. Best wishes with that. Maybe it's a curse? ☺

How I wish you would have lived in the amazing time I did. Greece and Rome, but especially Greece had such scholars, who challenged one another in public forums of debate. Many of us received Divine wisdom too but never divulged the source. We were happy to bask in the admiration of others.

This message was just to acknowledge you and your very impressive gifts and to encourage you to use them. Make the time, do impactful work [and] *don't just labor for a living. God will provide for you.*

I'll be watching and one day I will be with others who welcome you home. Socrates

This message from Socrates came twenty-five days later. He obviously wasn't finished.

Sandra,

I've come to you again to speak about wisdom. What it is and who is likely to have it. Wisdom comes when one has lived long enough to blend experience with knowledge.

Many confuse knowledge with wisdom, but it is not. Wisdom has a depth that many societies recognize, unfortunately yours does not honor. Ancient Rome and Greece, of course, but also most Eastern civilizations sought the counsel of their elders as did most indigenous people across many lands: your American Indian, many African tribes, and many tribes from South America recognized the value age brings to an opinion, on practically anything.

You are wise, Sandy, not only because your years are advancing but also because of your keen and advanced intellect. You are, indeed, smart. Couple the two, you are a valued friend and as a grandmother, wonderful. But, today, your society places its emphasis on youth, high energy, quick wit, and flash answers with no depth. So, your society of individuals have all become shallow thinkers. Where is the analysis? The strategy? The reasoning? At all three you are a master, which is why many of us here like using you as a vessel.

Try to encourage others to seek out those who have less to say but the most to impart. Wise people don't ramble on and on. They don't need to try to formulate a thought through talking. They know. And when one knows, sometimes a simple smile or nod is sufficient.

I know I surprised you with this visit and you had no idea what I'd possibly say. Well, it's not your job to know in advance, my friend. Have faith, listen, and write. ☺

It's an honor to speak through you, Sandy. Until next time, Socrates

NAPOLEON HILL

(1883–1970) American self-help author best known for *Think and Grow Rich*, published in 1937 and considered to be among the ten best self-help books of all time.

Great minds think alike. Or, rather, messenger souls often communicate similar sentiments. There are only so many truths about life, the growth of our souls, and how we should interact with others. It is the messenger who carries the correct slant or spin on it to fit the times.

These key communication strategies are re-interpreted throughout generations by various voices who are able to connect with their respective constituents. I believe Sharon Lecter is helping translate my latest publication [for] *a newer group who might not understand my meter and phrasing. A translator, of sorts. I'm most appreciative that my people found her.*

Hill is referring to his latest published work, *Outwitting the Devil: The Secret to Freedom and Success,* originally written in 1938 but held for publication by his family because it was thought too controversial. This newly released work is annotated by Sharon Lechter, who co-authored with Robert Kiyosaki *Rich Dad Poor Dad* and is a bestselling author herself. I read it and it truly is excellent.

You, on the other hand, have so many to speak for, so you cannot speak at all. You must only listen and transcribe. A tough job for someone as smart as you, my dear. But you are masterful, and we all feel very safe in your hands, which is why legions are lining up over here to make their thoughts known and somehow make an impact at a deeper level.

I am proud that you are a comrade in pen, more or less. Your original thoughts are much like mine and it would have been wonderful to have known you in a lifetime. Maybe next time around you'll be a publisher or agent or whatever one will call the person who gathers brilliance for distribution. Funny comparison, but you likely understand my intent.

Dear Sandy, thank you for taking time for me, for knowing, for understanding, and for being a pure vessel for our voices.

We all admire and love you, Napoleon Hill

I inserted Maria Montessori here because what she said was so observant and profound. Most importantly, she stands out because her message is so critical as she dwells on a subject no one else did. She'd have been lost in any other chapter and so this physician and educator brings her penetrative insight to the subject of our children, our most important resource.

MARIA MONTESSORI

(1870–1952) Italian physician and educator best known for the philosophy of education that bears her name, and for her writing on scientific pedagogy. She earned her medical degree in 1896 from the University of Rome.

Hello. Hello.

I'm delighted to be here and to be so welcomed by you, Sandy. Thank you.

This is all about our children! Don't forget them. In a world driven by power and greed, children [can] *get in the way. They become instruments to use. They become show pieces for advancement, for social acceptance, and for servitude—either in a practical sense or to our fragile and failing egos.*

Our children are our hope. The same as precious seeds in our garden of life. In the end, you will judge how healthy the garden you left not only your children but all children. Will the final plants be robust with their colors vibrant and their faces basking in the light, or will they be limp, weak, and smashed into the earth from being trampled on because their caregivers were hurrying to rush somewhere else?

Our children reflect the love and values of our societies. What have you all done to them? Think about the effects of this virus, the selfishness with which we throw them away as possibilities and the abuse we inflict as they become receptacles for our lust or vessels to be drained to benefit us. You will see the horror as I do if you stop and look.

Please remember yourself many decades ago (in your own life) and then remember the world's and your children today.

Thank you, Sandy. I hope you have room for this message. It may be the most important one. Maria

Maria's statement on what we have done to our children should be given a little time to read and digest. I will help with that, so the nuances are not missed. As she spoke, I saw clearly to what she was referring. In the first example, she cited how the needs of children have been ignored during the COVID-19 panic, the shutdown of schools, and the absence of social interaction our children were forced to endure. More importantly, many were kept prisoners in home environments which they often try to escape because of physical, emotional, or sexual abuse at the hands of their family. The only escape for many was attending school each day.

The lack of physical schooling also causes many to suffer nutritionally because the one good, balanced meal they may receive in school may be the only one they receive all day. Being physically in school represented safety and comfort for many who were stripped of that for twelve months or more. One day we'll come to realize that the unwarranted shelter-in-place policies did more damage than they did good, especially for our most vulnerable populations.

Maria also mentioned the selfishness with which we throw our children away as possibilities. This was a clear reference to the casual use of abortion, and how our convenience instead of any viable medical concern is most often the driver. Then, when she talked about using children as receptacles for our lust, that should be self-explanatory since child sexual abuse is so prevalent and pedophilia runs rampant in the global society. It's so tragic now that there is a movement to label pedophilia as a preference instead of an affliction.

Finally, when she made the "vessels to be drained to benefit us" remark. That might not be as clear to those who are unaware of the related satanic practices and harvesting of adrenochrome from natural origins [our children] instead of from a lab. The adrenalin from children facing death is thought to produce a fountain of youth effect, besides being an energy stimulant. Just because the thought of this is abhorrent doesn't mean such rituals don't exist.

I guess Maria Montessori has a much greater and objective perspective over there.

PLATO

(428/427 or 424/423 BC–348/347 BC) Athenian philosopher during the classical period of Ancient Greece. He founded the first institution of higher learning in the Western world, the Academy.

My dear child,

You seem a child to me because I've been gone for so long. I see you've had other great minds come. Ever wonder why? Because intellect is so lacking today.

Society has become numb to thought, to intellectual curiosity, [and] *to stimulating the mind. As you use your intellectual curiosity you are stimulating ours. Your fuel comes from receiving wisdom from the ages* [the other side] *but ironically, where did you think ours came from? Same place. There are only a finite number of ideas and although the number may be large, it is still a finite quantity. Where I am going with this is simply to make this point.*

When you open doors to new ideas and new worlds, people grow. They cannot grow in a closed space. This new assemblage of souls in the upcoming book will do that for readers. More so than a story or one thought woven even intricately with the language available. The latter often becomes repetitive and monotonous for the very bright. You, on the other hand, will keep them [readers] *challenged with a flash of brilliance, a unique perspective, a soulful reflection— that relates and so much more. Here and there, jumping around, to keep the spark of energy, intellectual energy, alive.*

Hopefully, people who read this book will know what to do as they proceed [in life]*: not accept everything literally and expect to* *be led to some predictable conclusion, but rather to stop, pause a bit, and absorb something entirely unexpected and worth absorbing.*

Good job, Sandy. I hope I lent something to your work, a valuable contribution. Fascinatingly, everyone's message is so individualized—not at all expected! This book will do all you expect and more!! [It will] *open humanity to the world beyond one with predictable limitations. Plato*

LAOZI (LAO TZU)

(Circa sixth century BC and fourth century BC) Also known as Lao Tzu, he was an ancient Chinese philosopher and writer. He is the reputed author of *Tao Te Ching*, founder of philosophical Taoism, and a deity in religious Taoism and traditional Chinese religions.

I am, no doubt, the oldest voice you've received. Interesting that you know nothing at all about me except that I lived hundreds of years before Jesus Christ came to teach as an extraordinary example of sacrifice and Divine living.

I have not returned as I was a master teacher who was given, like all of us, the thoughts to communicate to others. We received the inspiration and the words flowed. People listened to me, and I suppose I am here to bring some of my messages to today, where they will be grasped and hopefully applied. Will you do that for me? An odd request I know, but there are several quotes I'd just like to have repeated; and you can easily find them and know.

I want people to learn from less. Their thought process should take it from there. The one or two which relate, I hope will be of use today.

Wisdom doesn't fade with time. Pure wisdom is eternal. Laozi

I am more comfortable referring to him now as Lao Tzu since I didn't connect the dots when Laozi was identified as the person next wanting to speak. I really knew virtually nothing about Taoism but will be reading more once this book is published. I guess that's the beauty of giving all these souls a forum with which they can teach and share.

Now, to honor Lao Tzu's request. Here are the quotes I was called to deliver to readers. He has others that were equally or more famous, but these are the ones appropriate for this book. The perfect way to wrap up a chapter and provide fodder for more thinking and reflection.

Being deeply loved by someone gives you strength, while loving someone deeply gives you courage.

Nature does not hurry, yet everything is accomplished.

A good traveler has no fixed plans and is not intent on arriving.

When I let go of what I am, I become what I might be.

If you do not change direction, you may end up where you are heading.

To the mind that is still, the whole universe surrenders.

He who knows others is wise. He who knows himself is enlightened.

Chapter 20

MESSAGES YOU WOULDN'T EXPECT

This is a fascinating part of the book since the souls who speak here are not sharing topics that you'd expect them to communicate. In this case, predictable names are revealing thoughts that are completely unpredictable. Although many who preceded made unanticipated comments, the ones selected here were the most surprising.

FRANK SINATRA

(1915–1998) One of the most popular and influential music artists of the twentieth century, with one hundred and fifty million records sold. He is also one of the bestselling music artists of all time.

Well, you finally got around to Ol' Blue Eyes. Ha. Saved the best for last? I know you had a bunch of messages today and I am happy I was even able to get through. If I'd have been singing, you'd have let me in much earlier!

Well, Sandy, I'll bet you have no idea what I'm about to say. I saw Dean came to you. He was one of my closest friends, ever. He was fun, irreverent, and an incredible distraction from all that is difficult or challenging in life. He did that for everyone, especially me. Now, we are together, along with so many of the other Rat Packers. Boy, what a group.

So, I'd better get down to why I came. I lived life to the fullest; squeezed every bit of life out of this experience or vice versa. I had most of the women I wanted, sang the songs I loved, picked the best partners to deliver my music, and the best friends to share the stage. What could have been better? Well, a few things, I guess.

I wasn't a father I was proud of. I didn't spend nearly enough time with my kids, or my wife Nancy. She was still my anchor as a good wife is. She wasn't exciting or competitive or a challenge, but she was "home" to me and gave me a sense of security that I needed; actually, the kind of security every man needs. Picking a wife is a tricky thing. Some men pick them because they look good to others and to them, some for their sex appeal, some because they have no choice—an early pregnancy for example, and some because of peer pressure of some type—or pressure from the woman. Those are all dreadful reasons.

Pick a friend. You have to like to look at her and you have to find her attractive. Decent sex is good, too, but it doesn't have to be the kind that turns you inside out. That wears off in time. A good friend is loyal, kind, supportive, and dependable. Maybe some of those words are the same, but once you take a vow, you should really mean it. Work out the problems. Try to be faithful to each other and forgive. Your kids need the stability and two parents. No doubt about that. I was grateful for Nancy; she was the best.

My life was over-the-top though, and the way I pushed my music, chased woman, entertained twenty/twenty-four, and really lived an exaggerated life, I just couldn't be the perfect husband or father. I loved everything I did, acting came a bit later but I adored that, too. I was put on this earth to entertain, romanticize life, and stir emotions in people. I did that.

So, believe it or not, I was here to talk about the importance of a good marriage; especially for a man since I don't know the other side. I hope men who read this will take marriage seriously, take their time picking and pick one who you will be proud to introduce and be proud to have be the mother of your children. That's the best.

So, kiddo, I'm off to see what kind of trouble I can get into over here. ☺ Obviously kidding, but I had to lighten everything up a bit or people wouldn't believe it was me.

You're one decent-looking chick. A bit tall for me, but I still might have liked you. Much love, Frank

I had adored Frank Sinatra for decades and believed he was the most charismatic, sexy, and talented man in show business, but I never focused on any of the details of his life; especially how tall he was. So, after his comment about my height, I thought I'd look up his. Frank Sinatra was anywhere from 5'6" to 5'7½" tall, depending on the source of the information. He often exaggerated and said he was 5"9" or 10" or 11" but perhaps that was his height with the 2" lifts he also wore in his shoes, which I believe is and was pretty common with many entertainers, including Michael Jackson. So, since I am 5'9" and 6' in heels, I guess dear Frank was absolutely correct.

DINAH SHORE

(1916–1994) American singer, actress, and television personality. Chart-topping female vocalist of the 1940's and host of a series of variety TV programs for Chevrolet in the 1950's.

Hi Miss Sandy.

I still have that Southern accent! ☺ You got my name right away. I'm flattered.

Gee, life on earth is such a wonderful adventure. Not everyone who arrives here [Heaven] *realizes that. So much time with our soul work and when we see our life, the pain and imperfections stand out, but for those of us who lived a fairly balanced life—with a good amount of love in our hearts and no desire to ever hurt anyone intentionally—we see life differently.*

Time goes so quickly here yet stands still. Hard to describe. It can be many, many decades, or hundreds of years before we realize we might return. That's why so many of us are still here to communicate with you.

Sandy, my message is simple. Appreciate this amazing opportunity to live a whole life on earth or elsewhere! If you can't figure out a purpose, just try your best to be an example to others of sharing love, helping others, appreciating humor, and delighting in nature! Life will then place you where you belong. All the wonders God provided are there to experience in ways we cannot here.

Don't waste a moment! Love and live and laugh. Whoever put those three words together was genius. Express yourself through your gifts: how you use your hands, how you think, your personality, your creativity and so on. Bring blessings and joy to those you know.

Be grateful for this life because as magnificent as Heaven is, you'll miss the lows that exist to help us appreciate the highs. Life [on earth] *is wonderful.*

Just a reminder from little old me, Sandy. Dinah

When Mother Teresa came, it was nice to have another saint join Joan of Arc. I was surprised with Mother Teresa's comments regarding how the Catholic Church perceived her in the early years, and she them, before she officially left convent life and went out into the world to save the unfortunate children in India.

MOTHER TERESA

(1910–1997) Albanian-Indian Roman Catholic nun and missionary who founded the Missionaries of Charity with, in 2012, over forty-five hundred nuns active in one hundred thirty-three countries. Canonized as Saint Teresa of Calcutta.

My dearest child,

Tell Mary Jo hello for me and how wonderful Molly turned out. That was a very good placement.

Mother Teresa was referring to my friend, Mary Jo West, the "First Lady of TV News" in Phoenix, who adopted one of Mother Teresa's babies, directly from Mother Teresa. Her daughter, Molly, is now grown and a mother herself. It is one wonderful story.

Hello, Sandy. I guess you studied up on me a bit since you referenced some of your material on self-love and narcissism on my early life. Yes, people thought I had too much focus to be a good Catholic servant, since we served the rules of the Church first and people second. I was driven to the opposite of that, which was why I was always chastised or questioned. Never enough to be evicted from that particular house of God but routinely sent to my room—or be "grounded"—as you'd say today.

Finally, I found my home with the souls I was called to rescue. The need was so great. It took money to feed them and shelter them and pay for support people (never enough volunteers), so sometimes I was criticized for that (enthusiastic fundraising) too.

But, no doubt, dear Sandy, this was always your calling. Empowerment! Your own and for all those you touched throughout your life. Now even for ours on this side of things. For the first time, through you and Jon's relationship, do we see how our souls can be empowered in our own growth. Never imagined [that], *and then the two of you showed up.*

Stay well, take care of yourself. Rest today because you have so much work to do educating the world.

At this point, I thanked Mother Teresa for thinking of my health.

Always here to serve!! And you, my dear, are this love soul over there fighting this massive battle. (I'm) petitioning God to intercede on your behalf, especially on your health today.

I love you, my child. We all love you. You have no idea of the magnitude of that.

Signing off for now, Mother Teresa

Let me clarify, there was no major health issue at hand. I had just been pushing myself to the limits and was a little rundown with a typical bug of some sort waiting in the wings. It was no biggie, so I just relied on my natural antiviral remedies and got extra rest. I was back to normal in thirty-six hours.

J. PAUL GETTY

(1892–1976) American-born British petrol-industrialist who founded Getty Oil Company in 1942. He was the patriarch of the Getty family. In 1966 he was the richest living American, according to *Fortune* magazine.

My dear Sandy,

Not all rich men were monsters! Some focus on legacy not acquisition, quality not quantity, and beauty not power. I'd have rather sat in front of a magnificent piece of art than counted my money.

Achievement is nice, but accolades do not fuel self-satisfaction; that's achieved at a much deeper level and comes from within.

I hope people remember me for the beauty I left behind, not for where I may have ranked on a wealth list somewhere! My message is short and sweet. Don't forget to appreciate quality and beauty and true artistry! It's rare but it lasts forever.

J. Paul

I expect readers have all heard of the J. Paul Getty Museum, or the Getty as some refer to it, with its two locations: Getty Villa in Malibu and the Getty Center in Los Angeles. The Villa alone houses approximately forty-four thousand works of art from Greek, Roman, and Etruscan antiquities of which over twelve hundred are on view. The Center houses European paintings, drawings, sculpture, illuminated manuscripts, decorative arts, and photography from its beginnings to the present. An international collection. There is no doubt J. Paul Getty wanted others to enjoy the beauty he so obviously did.

ENZO FERRARI

(1898–1988) An Italian auto racing driver, entrepreneur, and founder of the Scuderia Ferrari Grand Prix motor racing team, and subsequently of the Ferrari automobile marque.

My dear woman,

What an exciting and romantic life I led; living in Italy was the start, since everything is romantic in Italy. The racing world was exciting and romantic as well, and I had an eye for beauty and a passion for speed. Look at the long life I was able to achieve. I loved everything about my life, and it was likely love that fueled the ninety years I lived.

I'm here to remind people to have a passion for something. Good food, fine wine, beautiful women, fast cars, fashion—it doesn't matter. It also doesn't matter if you work in that arena or not, as long as when you are around it, the passion soars and you feel fuller from the experience. Passion is life. If people shut out passion, they shut out love. Not good.

So, my message is brief but to the point. Open yourself up to experiences, lots of experiences. Sample the best, continue to live a life of exposure and welcome every opportunity to learn a little more. You don't have to be a student of a subject, just learn enough about it, be curious enough about it that you can tell the [develop a] *taste.*

It doesn't matter if you live in a poor area or a mansion, you can still find a sport you love, a bottle of beer that tastes better than any other, a woman down the street who is the best looking in the neighborhood. Appreciate that beauty. Enjoy the experience of being around such things or experiencing such things. If you do that, you will live a life that has few regrets.

Sandy, that is why I decided to come to you. You have passion, you know beauty because you have it, wear it and enjoy it. You are just the type of person I would relate to. Plus, you are fearless, another trait I had. Being without fear allows one to take risks toward ultimate success and to not shy away from exciting adventures that make one's blood flow and adrenalin rush. Exciting—life is exciting if you aren't afraid to live it.

This has been enjoyable, my new friend, my beautiful friend. Thank you for allowing me to participate.

With joy and in love, Enzo Ferrari

I'm embarrassed to admit that although I thought I knew a lot about Thomas Alva Edison, I did not until I did a little research on him *after* transcribing his message. As I mentioned before, I always must then look up the individual to find their birth and death year and the verbiage for a one or two-sentence descriptor to summarize who they were. With Edison I read more.

The reason I did more reading about Thomas Edison was because a couple of the things he said made me pause and question: *am I hearing this right?* Anyway, I wrote exactly what I heard and then read about him to see if the dots would connect. Of course, they did, as they always do.

THOMAS EDISON

(1847–1931) Described as America's greatest inventor, Edison was also a businessman. He is responsible for

inventing electric power generation, mass communication, sound recordings, and motion pictures.

Hello Sandy.

I'm glad I caught the last train to you so I could be included in your fine book.

Invention! Aha, what a world filled with simultaneous thought and individuals all clamoring to take credit. I may have been among them. Yet, what is truly original? One person inspires with a quick idea or musing and another runs with it. I suppose it's the one who reaches the finish line first who wins.

Two things were strange to me here. The train reference because he had nothing to do with trains, and I thought the metaphor was off, even though Edison was one of the last five souls who came for inclusion in this book. Yet, as I was glancing through his bio it seems his first job after his five years of school was that of a train boy on the railroad between Detroit and Port Huron. He was twelve years old at the time.

The other issue I had was his statement that he may have been among those who ran with the ideas of others and brought them to fruition. I recall something about the Tesla/Edison controversy and found that Tesla was part of Thomas Edison's "muckers," a group of like-minded engineers and inventors who gathered at Edison's massive laboratory at Menlo Park, where so many of his inventions were born. Fascinating how souls see their lives when their lives finally end.

I was bright (funny pun) and could see the detail that followed much like you often used to describe as the two types of people: the visionaries and the people who see all the levels beneath. You have all at very high percentages. Some are eighty/twenty, fifty/fifty or zero/one hundred, and so on. I was heavier on the mechanics and somewhat lighter on the original concept. I was still an inventor but the initial question of <u>How does this happen?</u> or <u>What if?</u> often *alluded me until I heard it* [first] *from a gardener, a woman, a colleague, or friend.*

Triggers are everywhere but those people never are recognized. Shows everyone the importance of relationships, connections, and collaborative work; however remote.

A confession? No. But a broader way to look at all genius so we don't become Gods, but instead very lucky humans with a path to follow.

Continue shining a light on life, thought, and possibilities, Sandy. You're quite good at it. —Thomas Alva Edison

Edison was unquestionably an incredible inventor. But in the outrageous rivalry between him and Nikola Tesla to bring electricity and innovation to the world, Edison was simply more adept at marketing his innovations even if perhaps Tesla was the true initial visionary.

If you didn't flip back and forth to this message after reading Nikola Tesla's message in an earlier chapter, now might be a great time for that. When reading both, because soul messages are always so true and free of ego, deceit, and defense mechanisms, the real story of the differences between the men surfaces.

Edison's final comment about how we all inflate the reputation of those geniuses among us makes total sense when you remember one of Edison's most famous quotes: "Genius is 1% inspiration and 99% perspiration." This might have been an attempt to broaden the field of credit often bestowed only on one.

Chapter 21

THE SIMPLICITY OF LIFE

We all remember the acronym, KISS, originally a design principle noted by the U.S. Navy in 1960. *Keep it simple, stupid* applies to life, as well – in how we should communicate, instruct, and critique.

Now neither the messengers in the chapter nor the readers of this book are stupid and that's certainly not the implication, but this refreshing chapter makes the lessons shared a very easy read. Nothing in this chapter needs much clarification and although the wisdom imparted is uncomplicated, don't overlook the value it might bring to someone overlooking the obvious.

FARRAH FAWCETT

(1947–2009) American actress, fashion model, and artist. Her red bathing suit poster sold eight million copies. She was married to Lee Majors and dated Ryan O'Neal.

Hi there, Sandy,

This is a treat. I was proud of my life although it was pretty simple: nice hair, good body, and pretty smile. The scripts I was given didn't require much acting talent, so, blessed with good physical traits, I had it made.

The one caveat: be at the right place at the right time. That's where destiny or one's life plan comes into play. This was supposed to be my life. My job was to not screw that up and I didn't. I was blessed in many ways.

Timing may be an issue for some, but other than the question of when, destiny is pretty much destiny. The real secret to life is how well you live your plan. With appreciation, humility, generosity, kindness, and love. Or other paths, which simply mean more time correcting those mistakes or oversights later.

Just a reminder that going through life with a smile and good energy makes even the most mundane existence memorable to others and very worthwhile to you. Not much wisdom, just more common sense. Farrah

John Wayne's message is totally logical coming from him. He was a man of few words and not a complicated thinker. In fact, his very basic approach to life is why I believe most people could relate to him and truly loved him.

JOHN WAYNE

(1907–1979) American actor who became a popular icon in western films. Known as "Duke," his career spanned the silent era of the 1920's through the Golden Age of Hollywood. He appeared in one hundred seventy-nine films and television productions.

Young lady:

I felt you reading about me in your friend, Rita's [Rita Davenport's] *book. Couldn't resist the opening. You're a bit like a magnet, you know. Some of us feel a familiarity, whereas sometime in your life you read about us, watched us, or remembered us and that opens the door. Other times, we see you being connected (on the radar screen—HA!) and either you, your work, or your energy draws us! You've got some power, kiddo.* ☺

Rita Davenport was initially a local television celebrity who became an international expert on the principles of success, time management, self-esteem, and confidence-building, besides being wildly successful in building an international network marketing company. An award-winning speaker and author of several books, most laced with her amazing humor, I've known Rita longer than either of us are old. I'm proud to call her a friend. Yes, a story about John Wayne is in her book, *Funny Side Up*, which I had read shortly before John's message.

I had a good life. I liked who I was overall. Not 100% perfect, but what I did suited me, [and] *in reflection I had a pretty easy time. Always regrets for omissions but for very few actions. I haven't thought about a return and not sure I'll do that now. Plenty of time. Endless time up here. Maybe I need to wait until some world needs another cowboy! HA!*

At this time, I asked him why he came to me.

Just for support and so I could be part of the chorus of voices up here supporting your efforts.

John Wayne wasn't much for endless dialogue, so his answers were sometimes short and sweet. I followed up by asking him if there was anything he wanted to share with folks still living.

Sure. Be true to yourself. Be honest with yourself about who you are and what you're doing. Most people delude themselves a bit. Drugs and alcohol help with that but if a person is truly honest and can look in the mirror each night and smile back at themselves (not in a smug or arrogant way) with sincere contentment for another day that made us proud to be here, that's all you can hope for.

Who did I help? Whose life did I enrich or make easier? Who did I make smile? Who did I comfort or just listen to? Those are the important things and if we can do a couple of those every day, we've got it made. We've mastered this life.

You've got a lot to smile about, Sandy. You're one of the good guys.

Your pal, John Wayne

It's fascinating that of all the messages and all the souls who came to share their wisdom, John Wayne and "Hot Rod" Hundley, the basketball player, had very much the same message. These two men certainly had different degrees of success but were both very uncomplicated souls. They lived life authentically and people seemed to be drawn to them. Perhaps it was their philosophy about life that made each so appealing.

ROD "HOT ROD" HUNDLEY

(1934–2015) American professional basketball player and television broadcaster. He was the number one pick in the 1957 NBA draft from W. Virginia University, later played for the LA Lakers, and eventually became the voice of the Utah Jazz.

I met Rod Hundley when he was broadcasting for the newly formed Phoenix Suns franchise in the mid-60's when my husband, Bob Cowen, was the public address announcer for the team. Soon after, Rod opened a popular sports restaurant in Phoenix when he was no longer playing basketball.

Hi Sandy,

Isn't this fun? Glad you remember me. All the time we knew each other I was just around the fringes of the Phoenix Suns. Not sure if I played when you and Bobby would be at the home games, but we all remember the restaurant I had on Central Avenue.

Gosh, I can't believe I can reach out like this. I think some people may remember me, but I wasn't terribly famous. Since I was a player [for the LA Lakers], *an announcer, and later a restaurateur, I guess I had some fans.*

I really did come for a reason. First, that you can really attract us like this (my first time communicating this way), and guess I'm a little excited but Connie [Hawkins] *brought me over since you talked to him. This is really wild.*

Gosh, to have the mic [microphone] *again is a big deal for me. HA! Not sure I'll know how to talk about myself, but I'll try. Gee, I was a big flirt. I don't think that really caused anyone any pain that I've just had to re-experience here, maybe just a couple winces from other women I was dating or married to at the time. Couldn't help myself. ☺ It's when I followed through and got caught, that was different.*

Other than that, I was an honest person although I grabbed a little cash out of the till (my restaurant cash register) from time to time, for a little extra walking-around money. Does this sound like a confession to you? HA! Don't mean for that to be, just wanted to explain that I had a pretty innocent and fun life. Guys liked me. Women really liked me. I kept it light.

Sandy, even God has a sense of humor. So, living life without all the drama and deep reflection isn't a bad thing, it's just not a productive or memorable life. I guess that was me.

So, I'm here just to say: be yourself. Believe me, God will still love you even if you don't move mountains in your lifetime. The only issue will be slow, slow soul growth if you're just in it for fun. At some point, your soul will have to master compassion, unconditional love, gratitude, generosity, and all the other values that make up perfection. That's the ideal end result and our souls won't truly be happy and can't rest until then!

Sandy, I hope you realize what you're doing! This is HUGE!! Allowing all these thoughts to flow to so many people. Someone will find one or two voices in this book that will change their direction, open their eyes, or help them heal. A little something for everybody and you don't judge, you just keep writing all our babble down. Amazing, kiddo.

Knew I always liked you, but you were taken back in the 60's and 70's. Too bad.

But now, here I am! A friend forever. Thank you!!! Rod

FLORENCE NIGHTINGALE

(1820–1910) English social reformer, statistician, and founder of modern nursing.

Well, I don't feel like I'm worthy to be in such company contacting you on this day, Sandy. Just a nurse. But I had courage and loved serving. Perhaps that's all one needs for a successful life.

Love what you're doing, at all times, in all stages and have the courage to step out when you're needed. People can feel when that is. It's a calling or a nudge or a small voice inside or when someone in need asks. Don't hesitate, serve.

I'm not a thoughtful soul, I'm just an ordinary one but somehow people remember me. Maybe now I can say something to still help and be of service.

Thank you so much for that. Florence

JOHNNY UNITAS

(1933–2002) American football quarterback who played in the NFL for eighteen seasons spanning from 1956–1973. He's listed as one of the greatest NFL players of all time and was inducted into the Pro Football Hall of Fame in 1979.

I was a football great, I guess. Anyway, I loved the game and never clamored for fame or any such. I was loyal, disciplined, and a real team player! We should be like that in life.

We don't need sports to be loyal to those we make a pledge to, to be disciplined in any effort which earns our way or keeps us in good health, and a team player in life. Help and watch out for one another always!

You can do that with neighbors, family, friends, co-workers, or even those you casually encounter at events or in your daily routine. Being a team player simply means do your part, act responsibly, watch out for one another, and treat each person as an equal; with love and respect, most of all.

Sports provides valuable life lessons and those of us who lived our life in one sport or another, we should share those values with others [and] *help educate them. It's a good way to live.*

That's what I've tried to do, Sandy. Thank you for letting me speak.

Johnny Unitas

DALE EARNHARDT

(1951–2001) American professional stock car driver and team owner who became an instant legend with he died because of injuries sustained in a 2001 Daytona 500 crash.

Dear Sandy,

I'm a patient sort unless I'm on the track, so was happy to wait a bit (for you). I know how busy you are and am grateful for this chance to say hello.

Being on this side of things now, all I can say is how glorious and magnificent Heaven is. The peace and love inspire all of us souls to want to rise to perfection since just existing in this environment is a constant reminder.

So many of us are ready or will become ready soon to jump back into a life experience to further learn and grow, but things are changing so quickly there. The energy, the awareness of evil, and the ability of so many living souls [all of you alive] *to increase your frequency or love quotient by means of awareness and ability to change now!*

Sandy, you can help people become aware of how that works. How to open to love and how to transform into more pure beings. Less time recycling to refine [our souls]. *And your book, this book, helps us, too, make some inroads not normally achieved from here.*

I probably don't sound like myself since everybody remembers me as a car and speed guy—my love and my life! And, for anyone who loves what they do one hundred percent, then dying in the sport, fits the bill. It was a perfect ending for me. I hope people realized that.

Now, here I am so different to everyone, but my core is identical. Throw yourself into life. Commit. Live. And you'll end up loving what you do if you do it for the love of the experience and not [for] *the fame and glory that comes.*

The right things will happen for your life path, but I encourage everyone to live full-out and squeeze every bit of joy there is from your work and life before it's over. Sad to see souls who come here with regrets; not of what they didn't have, but of what they didn't do.

You're my kinda gal, Sandy. Guess I got more informal at the end, didn't I? Love ya', Dale

I think most of us can relate to simplicity, to real and normal people speaking from the heart. But in this case, we're talking about soul-to-soul dialogue, which is even more intimate. With each message, I felt their sincerity and willingness to be of service, somehow. The ego was gone but the humor and personality remained and that was delightful. This chapter was designed not to impress, but to gather people together to whom everyone can relate.

Chapter 22

TOUCHING AND PERSONAL

Throughout this book I've been a little embarrassed to include many of the personal comments souls made about me, which included common interests or shared experiences, but I felt allowing that verbiage to remain might remind us of the perceptive capability souls possess. Besides, since I also make it a practice not to edit a word of messages from the other side, I had no option but for them to remain intact.

Wayne Dyer came to me five times between 2015 and 2021, and although his earlier communications had nothing to do with this book, I felt including some elements of the string would provide insight as to how relationships can develop between there to here. The parts I picked might also be beneficial to readers to reveal how my calling is received by those who've passed. To include every word, much of which was practical or tactical, would not interest readers and would have been way too lengthy, so key points were selected from the earlier messages from his soul-mail or spirit-mail to me.

Even though I didn't know Wayne Dyer while he was alive, since he has passed, he has become a mentor and huge advocate of my work.

WAYNE DYER

(1940–2015) American self-help and spiritual author and motivational speaker. His first book, *Your Erroneous*

***Zones*, was one of the bestselling books of all time with an estimated one hundred million copies sold to date.**

Sandy,

Welcome to my world! Now that I am over here, I can see more and understand more about people, life, and the mysteries of the universe. I like, no, I love, your energy, your strength, and your commitment to help others. Plus, we have a leukemia kinship. I'll help you any way I can.

As many may know, Wayne Dyer suffered from leukemia at the end of his life, and he eventually succumbed to that. I'd been a leukemia survivor once and was in the process of recovering for a second time when in 2015 the first of his messages came. I was doing workshops on health and healing, because even though I wasn't totally healed yet, I was almost there. I had a few self-doubts about some coaching I was being asked to do for others. I asked if I was competent enough to do all of this. Wayne replied:

Oh, my God, <u>yes!</u> You are too hard on yourself. Most gurus regurgitate the thoughts of others: ancient teachers, peers, patients. But you, my dear, originate, experience, and prove throughout your life the lessons we all must learn.

Smiling in the light, Wayne

Wayne came again in 2016 and in that particular message I asked him if there was anything in his previous life for which he had regret? This was his answer:

Yes. Taking better care of myself in the practical sense. I would have loved to stick around another ten years. I think had I been more diligent about preventive care it would have helped. The mind can't do it all, as you well know. And, you know things I don't about changing the date, how free will works, other elements of healing.

Really, Sandy, people don't realize how wise you are. As you age and still "glow," people will take you more and more seriously.

Have a great day and week, my dear cohort. I'll be waiting with great enthusiasm your progress. Go get'em girl. Your friend, Wayne

I'd best explain two of Wayne's comments about things of which he wasn't aware, but I was. Those being: changing the date and how free will works. The date changing is probably the phrase that would pique the most curiosity.

I learned with my first bout of leukemia that my end date was near and for some reason, I asked for Divine guidance to see if there was any flexibility with that. There was. The reason being that for 80 percent of people given a death sentence; they have the power to change an imposed end date. For the remaining 20 percent, their departure date is tied to their life plan, as their passing will teach lessons or give benefits to others through Divine timing. I was in with the 80 percent and the date I'd assumed was "it" was totally optional by doing all I knew to do to help myself. Once I asked, I realized that I had much more flexibility. Wayne was not aware of any of this but is now that he is seeing more options.

Free will is the other element that determines how healthy we age. Some choose to defer their will to others, believe prognoses, and live like victims, and some elect to honor their lives and fight to save its quality. Becoming empowered and taking personal action is always beneficial. I delve into some of this in my first book, *Get Well—Even When You've Been Told You Can't,* and I believe this was Wayne's point of reference. That book, by the way, I'm getting ready to prepare for a second edition which will include my last healing journey and will update data, since it was published thirteen years ago.

By this time, I was in the republishing stage of my last book, "*Hi Momma, It's Me.*" In fact, I had just finished reviewing the publishing agreement (April 2020) when Wayne paid me another visit. This is what he said:

> *Sandy, remember how powerful you are. See the potential. Embrace it and live who you were meant to be. This is your life and your son's soul. Do this for the two of you. Nothing else matters. One shot, Sandy. Go all the way on this one.*
>
> *Great book, more to come. Your pal, Wayne*

The force of having someone believe in you is even more powerful than believing in yourself. Since my son Jon had passed two years prior, I had no one left who supported me that way. Raised an only child, I had only half-siblings remaining, from my biological mother who lived in Minnesota, and some wonderful friends, but no true love interest. Jon had known me at a different level, even though our life relationship was challenged for over twenty-five years. Deep inside, Jon had an unshakable faith that I would always deliver results and never fail to make something work. That kind of belief in another is incredibly powerful.

Wayne returned for a check-in (August 2020) and was one who really stepped up to provide the kind of support I was lacking. Ever since, amazing voices from the other side have become available to fill those gaps in my life.

> *Yes, again it's me! Strange friends we've become, haven't we? I love this work of yours. I wish I had had the incredible connection with Divine energy you do, in my last lifetime! WOW. Something very special, my friend. I hope you realize and are grateful for this.*
>
> *Sandy, I hope you appreciate that I reach out to you. I was a very big deal! ☺ And people would love to have my approval.*

Because of his amazing, ongoing support, I included Wayne on my website (in italics so people would know he was deceased) as an endorser of my last book. This comment that follows refers to the photo of him I selected.

BTW, like the photo chosen for your website [of him]. *A good one.*

We'll be doing as much as we can from here: clearing energy, lending support, and smiling. My new friend, so happy to be part of your exciting life, Wayne

After "*Hi Momma, It's Me*" was published (November 2020), Wayne came again, this time talking about my new website and the blogs I had begun to write. After his first short comment, I mentioned how lonely it was to be a writer, which is the subject of the second paragraph.

Sandy, I think your blogs are great.

I know. [Being alone and being a writer is] *not for everyone but without the ability to pour my thoughts out, I'd have gone mad. Granted all my thoughts weren't as original as yours, at the core, but my spin was. It was my voice that was crying to be heard.*

I wish I'd have known you when I was first diagnosed with leukemia. I know you'd have helped me. We'd have made quite a professional team.

I want you to know I am still watching you, encouraging you, and spreading the word up here. The way we do that is just crank up the love or frequency when we're in touch and it reaches out to others so they might notice. Who knows? You've sure had some interesting folks show up.

Worthy of attention, you are. Well, 'night, my pretty friend. Sleep well and hang in there for the fast, sometimes bumpy ride ahead.

Big smiles from here, Wayne

What a blessing Wayne Dyer has been in my life. He doesn't visit often, but when he does it is profound for me.

This next message was a real shocker. Living centuries before, Cornelius Vanderbilt created such a legacy that his family was latter grouped with the du Ponts, Rockefellers, Mellons, and Carnegies as some of the earliest and wealthiest families in America. The stunning part is that this impressive figure was amazingly open, reflective, and humble in asking me for help. I know that sounds unbelievable, but one day I will reach out to him again to see if he is still interested in my assistance. It would truly be an honor.

CORNELIUS VANDERBILT

(1794–1877) American business magnate and self-made multimillionaire who became one of the wealthiest Americans of the nineteenth century. He built his wealth in railroads and shipping.

Hello Sandy,

I'm here because I was an exception to the rule if you compare my life to today's standards. I was self-taught, street smart, and had an extraordinary sense of timing. I was on my own while others were in fifth grade. I was a natural entrepreneur and was driven my entire life. In work I found peace, satisfaction, and my purpose. I built an empire.

There are so many entrepreneurs today that the environment is actually tougher. The regulations, the competition, the taxes—I had none of that so total freedom was the environment in which I flourished. Again, I became legendary.

Do I have regrets? Not really since work was the focus of my life and my true love. Everything else took second place and I guess people recognized that and were happy just having me in bits and pieces and enjoying the money I earned. The sad part, and there is a sad part, is I missed the love between people, all people. I see it here and am in awe.

I've not returned yet because I can't imagine how I could ever find a lifetime where love of work could be converted to the love I should have (for others). Perhaps you can talk me into that, Sandy! You are a teacher on love!! I would consider whatever you propose since you were quite good in sending lost souls home for a number of years. That takes some doing, so maybe you could help me. See the value of connecting with the other side?

I am feeling aware and appreciating but the motivation [to return] *is missing. I'm not in an elevated frequency and not driven by the need to grow that. This* [Heaven] *provides more love than I can recently remember. See my dilemma?*

So, my lesson for others is to 1) consider the value of love, 2) practice it on people you might care about, 3) keep it up. At some point the right teacher will come into your life to help you feel what you're missing, or help you turn your love for the inanimate objects or work/tasks/efforts into true, soul-based love.

Now, I hope I gave you something valuable enough for your book, Sandy, and I hope you'll welcome me should I come again for a more private coaching session. I was dead serious (catch the pun?).

You're a treasure and I value this connection. Until later, CV

This upcoming connection was personal and fun. When they were younger, my grandchildren would ask to hear "Grammy stories" and I loved to oblige. Once, I started to tell them a story about Jimi Hendrix but thought they wouldn't know who he was. My grandson, Charlie, said he certainly did, and that Jimi Hendrix was one of the greatest guitar players, ever. Charlie was maybe ten or eleven at the time. So, I recounted this story.

Back in 1967, my former husband and Poppa to the grandkids, owned a record distributorship, and in that role we routinely invited others to join us when we greeted performing artists as they arrived at their concerts. Afterward, sometimes we took the entertainer to dinner or whatever was appropriate. On this one occasion, Jimi Hendrix was in town and when his limousine pulled up by the performer's entry door, there might have been eight or nine of us in line to greet him. Hendrix and his entourage walked toward the back door of the arena and on the way in, he saw me in line, grabbed my arm and pulled me in with him.

Crowd members shouted to Hendrix that I was Bob Cowen's wife and that he couldn't take me. He let loose of me and the whole thing was just very funny. That was the story I shared with my grandchildren.

A week or so later, Charlie was in religion class at St. Thomas the Apostle grade school when he told the priest, having no idea in what context, that Jimi Hendrix could have been his grandfather. I can't imagine the stir that caused but needless to say, I selected my stories more carefully after that.

Fifty-three years after the concert incident, Jimi showed up with this message.

JIMI HENDRIX

(1942–1970) An American musician, singer, and songwriter. He is considered to be one of the most influential electric guitarists in the history of popular music.

Well, there you are. It's Jimi Hendrix coming to you now. Want me to drag you into another concert?

When I focus on your energy, the story about you and me stands out—funny. And you tell it well. Tell your grandson, Charlie, I would have been delighted to be his grandfather. Very funny, in religion class? Well, that wouldn't have been my most comfortable place in school. HA!

Bet you don't know why I came to you, right? You figure it's because of the story you tell. Well, that's how you got my attention, but that's not the reason.

I loved what I did in this life. I loved music and I loved the guitar, more than anything else. But the way I celebrated my passion and love was destructive, not productive. Just think, I could have influenced so many young Black kids to take up this instrument. There aren't a lot of Black guitar players (at least electric), and I could have been a positive role model had I stuck around a bit. But

I was stupid and my approach to life was a little is good, a lot is better. So, everything was in excess. Not healthy.

A person can't appreciate what they have or are doing if they are constantly jamming more into the equation. What starts out as fabulous is overshadowed quickly by shoving more and more on top of that and then the appreciation is lost. Greed is destructive, mainly to the person who is greedy. I was that way with everything, including women.

When I saw you, I just flashed my glance at the line, and you stood out. Maybe your energy and maybe your outfit and maybe your looks or body type and blonde hair, who knows? But you were a quick burst of energy and I grabbed it. That is what I did throughout my life and look what it got me. Fast burnout.

So, I have come to you today to tell you not to do that. Savor every minute. Don't always push through the praise or force your body to do more and more and more. If you are slightly tired, rest. The best life is the balanced life. You will live longer and be able to do more of OUR work if you handle your life and where you are headed in this new role that way. Got it?

Also, you can tell Charlie I appreciated him saying I was the best guitar player in the whole world. Especially cool coming from a young White boy.

Sandy, you're special and that is why we are all stepping up to talk to you, to give you support to share love and to share additional wisdom. I hope we aren't a pain in the ass for being too aggressive here. Now, you're getting multiples (of us coming) at a time. Big compliment, kiddo.

I'm not sure I can contribute much in terms of wisdom. I'm still deep into my own learning since I was a mess, but I am here to support you and just be another voice in the chorus of souls cheering you on. Thanks for letting me connect and for being open to this wonderful new dimension in relationships. We're proud of you. Your friend, Jimi Hendrix

BILLY GRAHAM

(1918–2018) American evangelist, prominent evangelical Christian figure, and an ordained Southern Baptist minister. He was one of the most influential Christian leaders of the twentieth century.

My dear Sandy,

I know this must be a surprise, but, I've come to you today to offer my support for your efforts and to bring additional energy and strength to your voice.

You are an angel of God on a mission. I'm sure of that. And it must be difficult to feel the weight of all that responsibility being a woman alone. And, my goodness, you're really alone, aren't you?

God has given you the strength for this and although you may not know it or feel it each day, it's there. He always brings to bear the right elements at the right time for the task at hand. I would have loved to have met you, Sandy. I'll bet you're a surprise to people. Where they expect quiet servitude and a humble heart, understated but prepared, instead what appears is a flash of brilliance, radiating with lots of energy, beauty, and intellect, as well as personality, especially for your age. Disarming, indeed. I'd love to have witnessed that firsthand. God does enjoy a good laugh, doesn't he?

I cannot add much to your wonderful work except to encourage you to push and push to get your book out there. <u>So</u> needed and will be so valued, once read.

My dear Sandy, I'm here for you, rallying whatever forces are at my disposal to help you scale this mountain. It's a big one, but I have a feeling you never shied away from a great big challenge!!! Good luck, my new friend. I'm sending love and hopefully will open more doors here for you.

You're a winner, young lady, and I'm proud to know you. Billy Graham

CONNIE HAWKINS

(1942–2017) American basketball player who played for the American Basketball League, (ABA), NBA, Harlem Globetrotters, and Harlem Wizards. He was affectionately called "The Hawk."

Sandy, Sandy,

Do you remember me? I'll bet you're surprised. I guess some of us are more aware of people like you so we can do this. Don't know. But I saw others you and I knew, and I knew you, so what the heck. Rod Hundley's here with a smile. Remember him?

I had met The Hawk when my husband was doing the public address announcing for the Phoenix Suns their first five years in existence. I interjected, after he took a breath, that I recognized his loyalty to the Suns and what a special person he was.

I tried to be loyal and thanks for the special part. I didn't have hardly anything to say except to remember you and Bob and little Jon. Now look! A really big deal up here. HA!

He just moves ahead doing his thing, like he has a job to do. Doesn't pay attention to anyone else, but that's a little strange in this environment. Most of us are in quiet reflection but Jon's energy seems more directional and active. Guess God has given him an assignment. You, too! WOW!

Anyway, I just wanted to say "Hi" and be recognized as one of your supporters or admirers up here. Boy, lots of them as you pop up in the energy field. Lots more see you than you touched or made an impression on. Paying off now.

We're all sending love and positive energy your way. Hope it helps your efforts.

Signing off admiringly, Connie Hawkins

Henry Ford, the next visitor, came to me before I put a good system in place to determine who was coming prior to their message beginning. The reason I had to implement such a process is because multiple souls would come at the same time, and it was too stressful flying totally blind. However, Henry Ford was the first and last to keep me in the dark until he was near signing his name. Then I saw a faint image, automobiles, and finally a name popped into my head and the signature flowed.

HENRY FORD

(1863–1947) American industrialist and business magnate, founder of the Ford Motor Company, and chief developer of the assembly-line technique of mass production.

I guess I am causing you anxiety because you don't know who I am, and I've never reached out to you before. Who I am is not important; what I am about to say is. I was famous. I was very, very successful, and I was very determined. Always determined.

You have now, in your life, amazing potential, Sandy, to rise above all the silliness that surrounds you: friends who need your energy and contribute little; time wasters and incompetents. You need to recommit to this venture all that you have and all that you know.

You are brilliant, attention-getting, and lovely. Your smile is charming, and you have managed to create within yourself all the characteristics you truly admired in others.

The joy of Aunt Minnie; the humor of Margaret Hance; the class and style of Jackie O; and the charm of Francis Carpenter. The brilliance is all your own and the light you shine is all yours, too.

The people Henry Ford mentioned are sort of a secret I had about a handful of women who, to me, were quintessential in representing one special trait. When people would ask who my role model was, I never had an answer because I had none. But I did have a few women who exhibited characteristics I would have loved to possess.

The first was my favorite aunt, Aunt Minnie, who was my adopted father's sister. She was a simple, uncomplicated woman who always worked and was just a spark plug in life. Of course, she was a flapper and loved fun. Everyone adored her and loved to be around her. She loved to tell stories and she laughed a lot until she died in her nineties.

Margaret Hance, as you read earlier in this book, was the first woman mayor of Phoenix. Her humor was subtle but such a natural part of who she was, that I found it to be her most irresistible trait. The people she served adored her.

Jackie Kennedy Onassis, everybody recognized for being classy and beautifully dressed in her traditional and classic style, which I also always preferred. She had amazing taste, or amazing designers, not sure which came first, but good taste and class can't be bought.

Finally, Francis Carpenter will be the one nobody knows. She was married to the son of one of the original du Pont siblings and was the mother of a man I dated for several years. Not sure I'd ever met a woman who was as charming as Francis, when she turned it on. She captivated everyone she was with, including waiters and maître d's in every restaurant in which she dined. She lived both in Nantucket and Palm Beach and was over ninety when she finally passed. She thought charm was the most important characteristic a person should have, and this woman had that in spades!

Well, I guess I can't have any secrets doing the work I do, since even Henry Ford can name the women that I secretly admired for one trait or another. It's good that I'm naturally a very transparent person.

You have amazingly high standards and I have come to reinforce to you how important it is NOT TO COMPROMISE those. Stick to your guns. With that smile no one will care. Your compassionate heart and insight are yours, too. That's why I came. You are on lots of radar screens up here, but you don't need applause, you need direction, and I think you'd trust me to guide you wisely.

Take a breath. Rest a bit. You are one in a million and I don't think you can see that. Why in the world would I mess around with a peon?? HA! You're the real deal, so stay strong, take care of you, and the message from me is: DON'T COMPROMISE!!!

My best wishes. I'm here for you. Henry Ford

JAYNE MANSFIELD

(1933–1967) American film, theater, and television actress, and one of the early Playboy Playmates. A major Hollywood sex symbol during the 1950's and early 1960's and was well-known for her "wardrobe malfunctions."

Hello, Sandy.

You don't know me, but I know you watch my daughter, Mariska, on TV often. I'm so proud of her. Much more successful than I was. I was just glamour and breasts—no real talent in that, only good genes.

Jayne's daughter, Mariska Hargitay, has been starring in the longest running television drama series, "*Law & Order: Special Victims Unit,*" since the beginning. Jayne was married to Mickey Hargitay, winner of the Mr. Universe Competition, along with a couple of subsequent husbands when she died in a tragic automobile accident. Her three small children were in the back seat; Mariska was among them. Mariska was then raised by her father.

I'm coming to you in laughter at your article [blog I had written] *about "Blonde Meditation." Very funny. Actually, quite on-point since over here there is no thinking, just instantaneous thought. Like you say, "in the moment." We communicate telepathically or energetically. The former with you and the later up or over here.*

I just thought it was cute and wanted to acknowledge you. Boy, you've made a bit of an impression here. Most everyone in the last couple hundred years is aware of you—clearly Ascended Masters are, and souls with something meaningful to say, or those who feel a connection with you or that you will help them.

I know how busy you are and how intrusive we've been, so I'll keep it to a short message. FYI, I was pretty smart. I just looked very dumb! ☺

From one blonde to another, with oodles of love, Jayne

Chapter 23

IRRESISTABLE INVITATIONS

I hope reading *Souls of Legends Speak* has been adventurous, enlightening, and even a little entertaining for you at the same time. This last chapter is meant to be the most intimate since it's designed to bring you full circle to the original message I always try to deliver; connecting across dimensions is not only possible, but also helpful.

For those who are spiritual or religious, connecting with God, Jesus, Buddha, an individual Saint, or even angels should feel and be very natural. But even for individuals who have a personal relationship with the Divine, reaching out to departed family and other loved ones might seem like more of a stretch. To others, it may even seem dangerous somehow. I respect people's strong beliefs and am not here to convince anyone of anything, but I will pose one challenging question. Every message in this book came from the other side, and I wonder if any of those messages struck anyone as dangerous? Probably not if you've made it to this last chapter. ☺ Which brings me to the reason for the theme of this final chapter.

Several of the souls who wanted to visit with us and share their wisdom, insights, and perspectives said they were open to more! Some would be very happy just having people relate to who they were, the struggles they faced, or the knowledge they imparted. They probably would like to be remembered fondly or even just remembered at all.

If you really related to a couple who came to visit us and are curious about them, you might watch an old movie or listen to music that wasn't of your generation just to experience more of what they did in this life. You could read a book they wrote, research them a bit on the internet, or you might just like to say "Hi" to a few of them in some other way, knowing they are really not that far away. A few opened the door to that possibility.

ERMA BOMBECK

Keep it up, Sandy. Fight the fight and help people learn that we're open to connect if they are. [It] *would be a shame to waste an invitation like that.*

Fondly, Erma

For those of you who arrived on the scene well after Erma passed in 1996 and may not know her, let me help with that. Erma Bombeck built a highly successful career as a brilliant humorist explaining to her throngs of followers, life through the eyes of a wife and mother. Erma was very funny with books such as *Family — The Ties That Bind… and Gag! The Grass is Always Greener Over the Septic Tank,* and *If Life Is a Bowl of Cherries, What Am I Doing in the Pits?*

She made the ordinary hysterical and helped shift many people's perspective from being bored with their very routine life to finding humor in it. Maybe Erma Bombeck is just the kind of woman you'd feel close to.

If not Erma, there are lots of other choices from legends who issued their own form of invitation.

RAY CHARLES

Anyway, I'm here. Happy to help, lend an ear, or participate in any way.

GOLDA MEIR

Meanwhile, we stand ready to be of service.

MARILYN MONROE

Please, Sandy, encourage people to open their hearts to us, to what we might be trying to say to them, or even to an individual in your own life who was important in some way. We'd love to reach out, but it's generally a very futile exercise.

It doesn't have to be futile if everyone would just consider that it's possible to receive and it's possible to communicate from here. The first step is always the most important. I think Marilyn would appreciate more friends who truly love and relate to her, even by just remembering or appreciating the candor of her message and learning from what she shared. I think that's the greatest compliment of all, and I'll bet she notices!

ERNEST HEMINGWAY

I'm grateful but I was a victim of my own vices and finally it all caught up with me—my demons and all. Now, at peace and with love surrounding me, I share what I can to be of service somehow.

Granted, Ernest was speaking about his sharing being of help to us, but I'll bet those who have a natural gift for writing, whether they ever publish or not, might relate to Ernest Hemingway; and if it was me, I'd have a chat with him, regardless. Nothing formal, just talk out loud like he was sitting right next to you. Not sure you'll receive any answer, but I'm sure he'll be listening.

MICKEY MANTLE

Now that I've been submerged in the bliss that exists up here and have had enough time for a slow learner like me to figure this all out (HA!), I want to give back.

How can anybody resist Mickey Mantle? Women my age will remember what a heartthrob he was when he was young, and baseball fans of that era will remember him, too. Seems like an irresistible invitation to me!

Another offered readers a direct challenge. That challenge sounded to me like a door being opened. Before you read that quote, here is a little reminder about the life of Rosa Parks.

Rosa Parks was a simple woman with strong principles who simply stood firm and refused to be a victim and to give in. No violence, no marching, just a simple gesture reminding others she was her own person. If you remember, Rosa closed by stating she and others like her had laid the groundwork for all citizens of this amazing country to step out, step up, and excel in their lives. She was advocating for positive action, not negative reactions. Although it sounded like she was speaking to the young Blacks in this country, I believe she was speaking to all the oppressed who need a voice.

Her closing comment wasn't a direct invitation, but I'll bet she'd love hearing from you if you are someone who faced the limitations of poverty or inadequate education and are still struggling with that state, or you're someone who is succeeding nonetheless! Instead of blaming others, you kept moving forward and became successful in terms of your family's history. Rosa Parks was that kind of person, strong in her values and determination!

ROSA PARKS

We all paved the way and now are watching you. Make us proud.

Others made indirect comments but so many were door openers, which I recognize because I've heard from so many souls over the last three-plus decades. Take for example, Paul Harvey, who appeared in the first chapter, explaining why these departed icons came to us all in the first place.

PAUL HARVEY

We're here to help and thank you for giving me a venue once again.

"Here to help" can be a very general statement or one that's specifically directed to you; it's your interpretation, but Paul Harvey isn't the only one. These additional souls were most eager to help since they are the ones who showed up.

As you know, many of these communication efforts will be more of a one-way effort but talking out loud to a good friend might really help you bring clarity to a situation you're facing. Remember how Lee Iacocca explained it?

LEE IACOCCA

As we speak through you, we gain more insight as to our own discoveries and imperfections. You know how sometimes when we're confused about a complex issue with no likely solution? Just talking out loud sometimes sheds light on the answer.

You don't have to have a "gift" to do that, you just need to be willing to vent to another person. If there is no one in your life who's a good listener without judging and offering their two cents of unsolicited advice, try communicating with God, Jesus, or Buddha, a saint, or an angel to whom you feel close—or even someone from this book! As Lee said, conversation, even one-way conversation, can be very healing even if you don't hear anything coming back.

This next message is a perfect reminder that for people searching for connectedness and love, it's all around us.

MAMA CASS ELLIOT

You can find what you're searching for by looking up (or over, HA1) and within. No need to become some monk. Just let Sandy open a couple doors for you and reveal the possibilities! Who knows? We might run into each other. Bye for now! Cass

Mama Cass wasn't the lead singer in the Mamas and the Papas, but she was part of something wonderful that needed the collective to succeed. Maybe you can relate to a life like that; maybe you can relate to her. Anyway, she's issued an invitation and so did many who preceded her. If nothing else, it's a wonderful sense of comfort knowing souls over there might have had the same challenges you are facing currently in life.

Billie Holiday's message was the most comprehensive and the strongest request for readers to connect with her and others, to express themselves, share common experiences, or just talk out loud to someone who might relate—whether they answer back, or not. That is why it is fitting we close this chapter and this book with her. These spirits always say what needs to be said much better than I do.

BILLIE HOLIDAY

(1915–1959) An African-American jazz and swing music singer. She had an innovative influence on jazz and pioneered a new way of manipulating phrasing and tempo.

Miss Sandy,

I'm probably before your time, or your interest in my music. I defined the blues, I think. I sang from my soul. I seemed to be able to clear my pain and any troubled feelings I felt through my music. People related.

I loved when I was on the stage and in front of the mic [microphone]. *Not for me to shine, but that metal instrument through which I'd be communicating allowed me to touch other souls.*

Now look at what you're doing. You've provided this gigantic microphone, which all of us can speak, sing, or cry into to help cleanse our souls, help others (maybe for the first time), and make a difference once again. I am so delighted you are now here, and I hope you won't grow tired of helping us communicate.

Perhaps this will make sense to folks. If you couldn't sing and express yourself that way; of if you didn't say much to others because you were unsure of yourself and your thoughts; or if the pain of sharing was just too embarrassing and devastating to even attempt, we are now here for you. Pick one of us and talk to us. You must relate to some well-known person who have passed. We're here. We're eager to connect and to help! We still want to serve while we are waiting to return for another lifetime, somewhere.

Thank God for Sandy and her openness, promotional spirit, and unconditional love for us all. She's like this spiritual matchmaker that simply opens the door to the possibility of coming together, and we push through to find our own way!

I hurt, too. I was lonely, too. Many of us in this book will be options for you and I'll bet most will be delighted to hear from you. We can't change your life, we can't give practical advice —unless you've learned to listen to us (and that takes a while), but we can listen to you.

Sometimes people just need an ear and to talk things out. They find their own answers through that if their dialogue is sincere. So, there! An open invitation.

God bless connections and sometimes the most unconventional ones are the best!!!

We love you all and we love you, Sandy. Thank you for everything, Billie

ABOUT THE AUTHOR

Sandy Cowen is an author, speaker, consultant, and personal coach who has experienced an unconventional life. Over her entire seventy-seven years, Sandy has been empowered and resilient. Initially, she was a self-made entrepreneur, who refined her marketing communication skills while building a fast-growing, under-capitalized business and then transitioned that business into a consulting entity that helped major companies across the U.S. and internationally—repositioning them for challenging marketplaces they faced.

Simultaneously, she was recovering from multiple chronic and life-threatening conditions—all without the use of pharmaceutical drugs or conventional medicine. That journey allowed her to write the first holistic handbook to help others navigate the world of alternative options to find the perfect answers for themselves. Her book was titled *Get Well—Even When You've Been Told You Can't.*

Finally, as someone whose spiritual gifts gradually appeared over a thirty-year period, she managed to hide them staying closeted as a reluctant medium until the passing of her only child, her son Jon, in 2018. It is then she wrote her second book, *"Hi Momma, It's Me.": How Souls Stay Connected Forever and the Power of Undying Love.* Today, Sandy and Jon, who would be fifty-two years old as of this writing, continue their relationship, although he is on the other side and she's right here.

With her third book, *Souls of Legends Speak: Surprising Reflections from the Other Side*, Sandy acts as a spiritual secretary capturing every word the icons who come willingly to her choose to share.

This empowering process helps them help others, once again. It also allows readers to peek inside these illustrious lives to gather their own insights.

Sandy Cowen, with her blogs and books, makes the life after accessible to everyone!

Made in the USA
Columbia, SC
08 November 2021